Praise for THERE IS A GOD

"In his youth, atheist Antony Flew committed to the Socratic principle of 'following the evidence wherever it may lead.' After a lifetime of probing philosophical inquiry, this towering and courageous intellect has now concluded the evidence leads conclusively to God. His colleagues in the church of fundamentalist atheism will be scandalized by his story, but believers will be greatly encouraged, and earnest seekers will find much in Flew's journey to illuminate their own path towards the truth."

> —Francis S. Collins, *New York Times* bestselling author of *The Language of God*

"A stellar philosophical mind ponders the latest scientific results. The conclusion: a God stands behind the rationality of nature."

> —Michael Behe, author of *Darwin's Black Box* and *The Edge of Evolution*

"There will be considerable interest in the clear and accessible account that Antony Flew gives of the 'pilgrimage of reason' which has led him from atheism to a belief in God."

> —John Polkinghorne, author of *Belief in God in an Age of Science*

"Anthony Flew has been for most of his life a very well known philosophical champion of atheism. He has now written a very clear and readable book tracing his path back to theism, revealing his total openness to new rational arguments."

> —Richard Swinburne, author of *The Existence of God*

"This is a remarkable book in many ways. It is always refreshing to find a major thinker acknowledging that he was wrong. But there is more. This book ranges without wandering. Its chapter on 'The New Atheism' puts Dawkins and Dennett in their place by a thinker they cannot dismiss as their inferior."
  —Huston Smith, author of *The World's Religions*

"This is a fascinating and very readable account of how a distinguished philosopher who was a militant atheist for most of his working life came to believe in the intelligent design of the universe, and hence deism. This book will provoke as much debate as his previous atheist writings."
  —Professor John Hick, Fellow of the Institute for
  Advanced Research in Arts and Social Sciences,
  University of Birmingham

"Antony Flew not only has the philosophical virtues; he has the virtues of the philosopher. Civil in argument, relentlessly reasonable, his lifelong quest for truth was implicitly a quest for the Guarantor of all truth. It is only fitting that this has been made explicit at last."
  —Ralph McInerny, Professor of Philosophy, University of
  Notre Dame

"Few religious stories have had such an impact. This amazing volume documents the reasons for Tony's change … and makes this delightful book absolutely required reading."
  —Gary Habermas, Distinguished Research Professor and
  Chair, Department of Philosophy and Theology, Liberty
  University

"Antony Flew's *There Is a God* is a fascinating record of how one of our most prominent contemporary atheists was led to the conviction that God does exist. The narrative is eloquent testimony to Flew's openness of mind, fairness, and intellectual integrity. It will come as a most uncomfortable jolt to those who were once his fellow atheists."

—Nicholas Wolterstorff, Noah Porter Professor Emeritus of Philosophical Theology, Yale University

"When Antony Flew, in the spirit of free-thinking, followed the evidence where he thought it led, namely, to theism, he was roundly denounced by supposed free-thinkers in the severest of terms. He had, it seemed, committed the unpardonable sin. Now we have the personal narrative of his journey from anti-theism to theism. I commend it to all truly open-minded seekers after truth."

—Dr. William Lane Craig, Research Professor, Talbot School of Theology

"Antony Flew's book will incense atheists who suppose (erroneously) that science proves there is no God. Flew is a distinguished philosopher whose position has been changed by force of argument about the significance of scientific discoveries. This engaging personal retrospective on Flew's philosophical pilgrimage illustrates that it is dangerous for an atheist to think too hard about his religious commitment—he might become unconvinced."

—Ian H. Hutchinson, Professor and Head of the Department of Nuclear Science and Engineering, MIT

"In *There Is A God* one of the leading analytical philosophers of the twentieth century shares with readers an intellectual pilgrimage that begins with healthy and principled skepticism and culminates in a theism based on rational warrants and a willingness to accept the evidence as given. Perhaps what provides the deepest satisfaction in reading this philosophical memoir is the author's transparent integrity, so habitual over a productive lifetime as to be, as Aristotle would have it, second nature. How shrill and self-absorbed are the opposing works of a Dawkins or a Dennett by comparison. Though written in a different part of the metaphysical register than Newman's *Apologia,* Professor Flew's exposition will be a source for reflective inquiry for many, many years. In his youth he was led by brave Socrates. Now older, he will serve as a model for others."

—Daniel N. Robinson, Philosophy Department,
Oxford University

THERE IS A
GOD

THERE IS A
GOD

How the World's
Most Notorious Atheist
Changed His Mind

Antony Flew

with Roy Abraham Varghese

HarperOne
An Imprint of HarperCollinsPublishers

HarperOne

Grateful acknowledgment is given to the following for permission to reprint their work:

Roy Abraham Varghese, "Preface," copyright © 2007, Roy Abraham Varghese.

Roy Abraham Varghese, "The 'New Atheism': A Critical Appraisal of Dawkins, Dennett, Wolpert, Harris, and Stenger," copyright © 2007, Roy Abraham Varghese.

N. T. Wright, "The Self-Revelation of God in Human History: A Dialogue on Jesus with N. T. Wright," copyright © 2007, N. T. Wright.

FIRST HARPERCOLLINS PAPERBACK EDITION PUBLISHED IN 2008

Library of Congress Cataloging-in-Publication Data
Flew, Antony
There is a God : how the world's most notorious atheist changed his mind / Antony Flew ; with Roy Abraham Varghese. — 1st ed.
p. cm.
ISBN 978-0-06-133530-3
1. Flew, Antony, 1923– 2. Spiritual biography—England.
3. Atheists—England—Biography. 4. Philosophers—England—Biography.
I. Varghese, Roy Abraham. II. Title.
BL73.F54A3 2007
212.092—dc22   2007019262

23 24 25 26 27 LBC 36 35 34 33 32

CONTENTS

PREFACE

Roy Abraham Varghese

"Famous Atheist Now Believes in God: One of World's Leading Atheists Now Believes in God, More or Less, Based on Scientific Evidence." This was the headline of a December 9, 2004, Associated Press story that went on to say: "A British philosophy professor who has been a leading champion of atheism for more than a half century has changed his mind. He now believes in God more or less based on scientific evidence, and says so on a video released Thursday." Almost immediately, the announcement became a media event touching off reports and commentaries around the globe on radio and TV, in newspapers and on Internet sites. The story gained such momentum that AP put out two subsequent releases relating to the original announcement. The subject of the story and of much subsequent speculation was Professor Antony Flew, author of over thirty professional philosophical works that helped set the agenda for atheism for half a century. In fact, his "Theology and Falsification," a paper first presented at a 1950 meeting of the Oxford University Socratic Club chaired by C. S. Lewis, became the most widely reprinted philosophical publication of the last century. Now, for the first time, he gives an account of the arguments and evidence that led him to change his mind. This book, in a sense, represents the rest of the story.

I played a small part in the AP story because I had helped organize the symposium and resulting video in which Tony Flew announced what he later humorously referred to as his "conversion." In fact, from 1985, I had helped organize several conferences at which he had made the case for atheism. So this work is personally the culmination of a journey begun two decades ago.

Curiously, the response to the AP story from Flew's fellow atheists verged on hysteria. One atheist Web site tasked a correspondent with giving monthly updates on Flew's falling away from the true faith. Inane insults and juvenile caricatures were common in the freethinking blogosphere. The same people who complained about the Inquisition and witches being burned at the stake were now enjoying a little heresy hunting of their own. The advocates of tolerance were not themselves very tolerant. And, apparently, religious zealots don't have a monopoly on dogmatism, incivility, fanaticism, and paranoia.

But raging mobs cannot rewrite history. And Flew's position in the history of atheism transcends anything that today's atheists have on offer.

FLEW'S SIGNIFICANCE IN THE
HISTORY OF ATHEISM

It is not too much to say that within the last hundred years, no mainstream philosopher has developed the kind of systematic, comprehensive, original, and influential exposition of atheism that is to be found in Antony Flew's fifty years of antitheological writings. Prior to Flew, the major apologias for atheism were those of Enlightenment thinkers like David Hume and the nineteenth-century German philosophers Arthur Schopenhauer, Ludwig Feuerbach, and Friedrich Nietzsche.

But what about Bertrand Russell (who maintained rather implausibly that he was technically an agnostic, although he was an atheist in practice), Sir Alfred Ayer, Jean-Paul Sartre, Albert Camus, and Martin Heidegger, all of whom were twentieth-century atheists well before Flew began writing? In Russell's case, it is quite obvious that he did not produce anything beyond a few polemical pamphlets on his skeptical views and his disdain for organized religion. His *Religion and Science* and *Why I Am Not a Christian* were simply anthologies of articles—he produced no systematic philosophy of religion. At best, he drew attention to the problem of evil and sought to refute traditional arguments for God's existence without generating any new arguments of his own. Ayer, Sartre, Camus, and Heidegger have this in common: their focus was on generating a specific way of engaging in philosophical discussion, an aftereffect of which was the denial of God. They had their own systems of thought of which atheism was a by-product. You had to buy into their systems to buy into their atheism. The same might be said of later nihilists like Richard Rorty and Jacques Derrida.

Of course, there were major philosophers of Flew's generation who were atheists; W. V. O. Quine and Gilbert Ryle are obvious instances. But none took the step of developing book-length arguments to support their personal beliefs. Why so? In many instances, professional philosophers in those days were disinclined to dirty their delicate hands by indulging in such popular, even vulgar, discussions. In other cases, the motive was prudence.

Certainly, in later years, there were atheist philosophers who critically examined and rejected the traditional arguments for God's existence. These range from Paul Edwards, Wallace Matson, Kai Nielsen, and Paul Kurtz to J. L. Mackie, Richard Gale, and Michael Martin. But their works did not change the agenda and framework of discussion the way Flew's innovative publications did.

Where does the originality of Flew's atheism lie? In "Theology and Falsification," *God and Philosophy,* and *The Presumption of Atheism,* he developed novel arguments against theism that, in some respects, laid out a road map for subsequent philosophy of religion. In "Theology and Falsification" he raised the question of how religious statements can make meaningful claims (his much-quoted expression "death by a thousand qualifications" captures this point memorably); in *God and Philosophy* he argued that no discussion on God's existence can begin until the coherence of the concept of an omnipresent, omniscient spirit had been established; in *The Presumption of Atheism* he contended that the burden of proof rests with theism and that atheism should be the default position. Along the way, he of course analyzed the traditional arguments for God's existence. But it was his reinvention of the frames of reference that changed the whole nature of the discussion.

In the context of all of the above, Flew's recent rejection of atheism was clearly a historic event. But it is little known that, even in his atheist days, Flew had, in a sense, opened the door to a new and revitalized theism.

FLEW, LOGICAL POSITIVISM, AND THE REBIRTH OF RATIONAL THEISM

Here's the paradox. By defending the legitimacy of discussing theological claims and challenging philosophers of religion to elucidate their assertions, Flew facilitated the rebirth of rational theism in analytic philosophy after the dark days of logical positivism. A little background information will be of value here.

Logical positivism, as some might remember, was the philosophy introduced by a European group called the Vienna Circle in the early 1920s and popularized by A. J. Ayer in the English-speaking world with his 1936 work *Language, Truth and Logic*. According to the logical positivists, the only meaningful statements were those capable of being verified through sense experience or true simply by virtue of their form and the meaning of the words used. Thus a statement was meaningful if its truth or falsehood could be verified by empirical observation (e.g., scientific study). The statements of logic and pure mathematics were tautologies; that is, they were true by definition and were simply ways of using symbols that did not express any truth about the world. There was nothing else that could be known or coherently discussed. At the heart of logical positivism was the verification principle, the claim that the meaning of a proposition consists in its verification. The result was that the only meaningful statements were those used in science, logic, or mathematics. Statements in metaphysics, religion, aesthetics, and ethics were literally meaningless, because they could not be verified by empirical methods. They were neither valid nor invalid. Ayer said that it was just as absurd to be an atheist as to be a theist, since the statement "God exists" simply has no meaning.

Today many introductory works of philosophy associate Flew's approach in "Theology and Falsification" with Ayer's kind of logical positivist assault on religion, since both question the meaningfulness of religious statements. The problem with this picture is that it does not in any way reflect Flew's own understanding of the matter then or now. In fact, far from buttressing the positivist view of religion, Flew considered his paper as a final nail in the coffin of that particular way of doing philosophy.

In a 1990 presentation I organized on the fortieth anniversary of the publication of "Theology and Falsification," Flew stated:

As an undergraduate I had become increasingly frustrated and exasperated by philosophical debates which seemed always to revert to, and never to move forward from, the logical positivism most brilliantly expounded in ... *Language, Truth and Logic*.... The intention in both these papers [the versions of "Theology and Falsification" first presented at the Socratic Club and then published in *University*] was the same. Instead of an arrogant announcement that everything which any believer might choose to say is to be ruled out of consideration a priori as allegedly constituting a violation of the supposedly sacrosanct verification principle—here curiously maintained as a secular revelation—I preferred to offer a more restrained challenge. Let the believers speak for themselves, individually and severally.

The story is taken up in the present work, where Flew comments again on the provenance of his celebrated paper:

> During my last term at the University of Oxford, the publication of A. J. Ayer's book *Language, Truth and Logic* had persuaded many members of the Socratic Club that the Ayerian heresy of logical positivism—the contention that all religious propositions are without cognitive significance—had to be refuted. The first and only paper I ever read to the Socratic Club, "Theology and Falsification," provided what I then considered to be a sufficient refutation. I believed I had achieved a total victory and there was no room for further debate.

As any history of philosophy will show, logical positivism did indeed come to grief by the 1950s because of its internal inconsistencies. In fact, Sir Alfred Ayer himself, in a contribution to an anthology I edited, stated: "Logical positivism died a long time ago. I don't think much of *Language, Truth and Logic* is true. I think it is full of mistakes. I think it was an important book in its time because

it had a kind of cathartic effect.... But when you get down
to detail, I think it's full of mistakes which I spent the last
fifty years correcting or trying to correct."[1]

At any rate, the departure of logical positivism and Flew's
new rules of engagement gave a fresh impetus to philosophical theism. Numerous major works of theism in the analytic
tradition have since been written by Richard Swinburne,
Alvin Plantinga, Peter Geach, William P. Alston, George
Mavrodes, Norman Kretzmann, James F. Ross, Peter Van
Inwagen, Eleonore Stump, Brian Leftow, John Haldane,
and many others over the last three decades. Not a few of
these address issues such as the meaningfulness of assertions about God, the logical coherence of the divine attributes, and the question of whether belief in God is properly
basic—precisely the issues raised by Flew in the discussion
he sought to stimulate. The turn toward theism was highlighted in a *Time* magazine cover story in April 1980: "In a
quiet revolution in thought and argument that hardly anyone would have foreseen only two decades ago, God is making a comeback. Most intriguingly this is happening ... in
the crisp intellectual circles of academic philosophers."[2]

THE "NEW ATHEISM," OR POSITIVISM REDUX

In the light of this historical progression, the sudden
emergence of what has been called the "new atheism"

is of particular interest. The year of the "new atheism" was 2006 (the phrase was first used by *Wired* magazine in November 2006). From Daniel Dennett's *Breaking the Spell* and Richard Dawkins's *The God Delusion* to Lewis Wolpert's *Six Impossible Things Before Breakfast,* Victor Stenger's *The Comprehensible Cosmos,* and Sam Harris's *The End of Faith* (published in 2004, but the sequel to which, *Letter to a Christian Nation,* came out in 2006), the exponents of a look-back-in-anger, take-no-prisoners type of atheism were out in force. What was significant about these books was not their level of argument—which was modest, to put it mildly—but the level of visibility they received both as best sellers and as a "new" story discovered by the media. The "story" was helped even further by the fact that the authors were as voluble and colorful as their books were fiery.

The chief target of these books is, without question, organized religion of any kind, time, or place. Paradoxically, the books themselves read like fundamentalist sermons. The authors, for the most part, sound like hellfire-and-brimstone preachers warning us of dire retribution, even of apocalypse, if we do not repent of our wayward beliefs and associated practices. There is no room for ambiguity or subtlety. It's black and white. Either you are with us all the way or one with the enemy. Even eminent thinkers who express some sympathy for the other side are denounced as traitors. The evangelists themselves are courageous souls preaching their message in the face of imminent martyrdom.

But how do these works and authors fit into the larger philosophical discussion on God of the last several decades? The answer is they don't.

In the first place, they refuse to engage the real issues involved in the question of God's existence. None of them even address the central grounds for positing a divine reality (Dennett spends seven pages on the arguments for God's existence, Harris none). They fail to address the issue of the origins of the rationality embedded in the fabric of the universe, of life understood as autonomous agency, and of consciousness, conceptual thought, and the self. Dawkins talks of the origins of life and consciousness as "one-off" events triggered by an "initial stroke of luck."[3] Wolpert writes: "I have purposely [!] avoided any discussion of consciousness, which still remains mostly poorly understood."[4] About the origin of consciousness, Dennett, a die-hard physicalist, once wrote, "and then a miracle happens."[5] Neither do any of these writers present a plausible worldview that accounts for the existence of a "law-abiding," life-supporting, and rationally accessible universe.

Second, they show no awareness of the fallacies and muddles that led to the rise and fall of logical positivism. Those who ignore the mistakes of history will have to repeat them at some point. Third, they seem entirely unaware of the massive corpus of works in analytic philosophy of religion or the sophisticated new arguments generated within philosophical theism.

It would be fair to say that the "new atheism" is nothing less than a regression to the logical positivist philosophy that was renounced by even its most ardent proponents. In fact, the "new atheists," it might be said, do not even rise to logical positivism. The positivists were never so naive as to suggest that God could be a scientific hypothesis—they declared the concept of God to be meaningless precisely because it was not a scientific hypothesis. Dawkins, on the other hand, holds that "the presence or absence of a creative super-intelligence is unequivocally a scientific question."[6] This is the kind of comment of which we say it is not even wrong! In Appendix A, I seek to show that our immediate experience of rationality, life, consciousness, thought, and the self militate against every form of atheism, including the newest.

But two things must be said here about certain comments by Dawkins that are directly relevant to the present book. After writing that Bertrand Russell "was an exaggeratedly fair-minded atheist, over-eager to be disillusioned if logic seemed to require it," he adds in a footnote: "We might be seeing something similar today in the over-publicized tergiversation of the philosopher Antony Flew, who announced in his old age that he had been converted to belief in some sort of deity (triggering a frenzy of eager repetition all around the Internet). On the other hand, Russell was a great philosopher. Russell won the Nobel Prize."[7] The puerile petulance of the contrast with the "great philosopher" Russell and the contemptible reference to Flew's "old age" are par for the course in Dawkins's epistles to the enlightened. But what is interesting here is Dawkins's choice of words, one by which he unwittingly reveals the way his mind works.

Tergiversation means "apostasy." So Flew's principal sin was that of apostatizing from the faith of the fathers. Dawkins himself has elsewhere confessed that his atheistic view of the universe is based on faith. When asked by the Edge Foundation, "What do you believe is true even though you cannot prove it?" Dawkins replied: "I believe that all life, all intelligence, all creativity and all 'design' anywhere in the universe, is the direct or indirect product of Darwinian natural selection. It follows that design comes late in the universe, after a period of Darwinian evolution. Design cannot precede evolution and therefore cannot underlie the universe."[8] At bottom, then, Dawkins's rejection of an ultimate Intelligence is a matter of belief without proof. And like many whose beliefs are based on blind faith, he cannot tolerate dissent or defection.

With regard to Dawkins's approach to the rationality underlying the universe, the physicist John Barrow observed in a discussion: "You have a problem with these ideas, Richard, because you're not really a scientist. You're a biologist." Julia Vitullo-Martin notes that for Barrow biology is little more than a branch of natural history. "Biologists," says Barrow, "have a limited, intuitive understanding of complexity. They're stuck with an inherited conflict from the nineteenth century, and are only interested in outcomes, in what wins out over others. But outcomes tell you almost nothing about the laws that govern the universe."[9]

Dawkins's intellectual father seems to be Bertrand Russell. He talks about how he was "inspired … at the age of about sixteen"[10] by Russell's 1925 essay "What I Believe." Russell was a determined opponent of organized religion, and this makes him a role model for Harris and Dawkins; stylistically too they emulate Russell's penchant for sarcasm, caricature, flippancy, and exaggeration. But Russell's rejection of God was not motivated just by intellectual factors. In *My Father, Bertrand Russell,* his daughter, Katharine Tait, writes that Russell was not open to any serious discussion of God's existence: "I could not even talk to him about religion." Russell was apparently turned off by the kind of religious believers he had encountered. "I would have liked to convince my father that I had found what he had been looking for, the ineffable something he had longed for all his life. I would have liked to persuade him that the search for God does not have to be vain. But it was hopeless. He had known too many blind Christians, bleak moralists who sucked the joy from life and persecuted their opponents; he would never have been able to see the truth they were hiding."

Tait, nevertheless, believes that Russell's "whole life was a search for God.... Somewhere at the back of my father's mind, at the bottom of his heart, in the depths of his soul, there was an empty space that had once been filled by God, and he never found anything else to put in it." He had the "ghostlike feeling of not belonging, of having no home in this world."[11] In a poignant passage, Russell once said: "Nothing can penetrate the loneliness of the human heart except the highest intensity of the sort of love the religious teachers have preached."[12] You would be hard put to find any passage that remotely resembles this in Dawkins.

Returning to the account of Flew's "tergiversation," it has perhaps never occurred to Dawkins that philosophers, whether great or less well known, young or old, change their minds based on the evidence. He might be disappointed that they are "over-eager to be disillusioned if logic seemed to require it," but then again they are guided by logic, not by fear of tergiversation.

Russell, in particular, was so fond of tergiversation that another celebrated British philosopher, C. D. Broad, once said, "As we all know, Mr. Russell produces a different system of philosophy every few years."[13] There have been other instances of philosophers changing their mind on the basis of evidence. We have already observed that Ayer disavowed the positivism of his youth. Another example of one who underwent such radical change is J. N. Findlay, who argued, in Flew's 1955 book *New Essays in Philosophical Theology*,[14] that God's existence can be disproved—but then reversed himself in his 1970 work *Ascent to the Absolute*. In the latter and subsequent books, Findlay argues that mind, reason, intelligence, and will culminate in God, the self-existent, to whom is owed worship and unconditional self-dedication.

Dawkins's "old age" argument (if it can be called that) is a strange variation of the ad hominem fallacy that has no place in civilized discourse. True thinkers evaluate arguments and weigh the evidence without regard to the proponent's race, sex, or age.

Another persistent theme in Dawkins's book, and in those of some of the other "new atheists," is the claim that no scientist worth his or her salt believes in God. Dawkins, for instance, explains away Einstein's statements about God as metaphorical references to nature. Einstein himself, he says, is at best an atheist (like Dawkins) and at worst a pantheist. But this bit of Einsteinian exegesis is patently dishonest. Dawkins references only quotes that show Einstein's distaste for organized and revelational religion. He deliberately leaves out not just Einstein's comments about his belief in a "superior mind" and a "superior reasoning power" at work in the laws of nature, but also Einstein's specific denial that he is either a pantheist or an atheist. (This deliberate distortion is rectified in this book.)

More recently, when asked on a visit to Jerusalem if he believed in the existence of God, the famous theoretical physicist Stephen Hawking is reported to have replied that he did "believe in the existence of God, but that this Divine force established the laws of nature and physics and after that does not enter to control the world."[15] Of course, many other great scientists of modern times such as Heisenberg and Planck believed in a divine Mind on rational grounds. But this too is whitewashed out of Dawkins's account of scientific history.

Dawkins, in fact, belongs to the same peculiar club of popular science writers as Carl Sagan and Isaac Asimov from a previous generation. These popularizers saw themselves not simply as scribes, but as high priests. Like Dawkins, they took on themselves the task not just of educating the public on the findings of science, but also of deciding what it is permissible for the scientific faithful to believe on matters metaphysical. But let us be clear here. Many of the greatest scientists saw a direct connection between their scientific work and their affirmation of a "superior mind," the Mind of God. Explain it how you will, but this is a plain fact that the popularizers with their own agendas cannot be allowed to hide. About positivism, Einstein in fact said, "I am not a positivist. Positivism states that what cannot be observed does not exist. This conception is scientifically indefensible, for it is impossible to make valid affirmations of what people 'can' or 'cannot' observe. One would have to say 'only what we observe exists,' which is obviously false."[16]

If they want to discourage belief in God, the popularizers must furnish arguments in support of their own atheistic views. Today's atheist evangelists hardly even try to argue their case in this regard. Instead, they train their guns on well-known abuses in the history of the major world religions. But the excesses and atrocities of organized religion have no bearing whatsoever on the existence of God, just as the threat of nuclear proliferation has no bearing on the question of whether $E = mc^2$.

So does God exist? What about the arguments of atheists old and new? And what bearing does modern science have on the matter? By a striking coincidence, at this particular moment in intellectual history when the old positivism is back in vogue, the same thinker who helped end its reign a half century ago returns to the battlefield of ideas to answer these very questions.

INTRODUCTION

Ever since the announcement of my "conversion" to deism, I have been asked on numerous occasions to provide an account of the factors that led me to change my mind. In a few subsequent articles and in the new introduction to the 2005 edition of my *God and Philosophy*, I drew attention to recent works relevant to the ongoing discussion on God, but I did not elaborate further on my own views. I have now been persuaded to present here what might be called my last will and testament. In brief, as the title says, I now believe there is a God!

The subtitle, "How the World's Most Notorious Atheist Changed His Mind," was not my own invention. But it is one I am happy to employ, for the invention and employment of apt yet arresting titles is for Flews something of a family tradition. My theologian father once edited a collection of essays by himself and some of his former students and gave to this polemic paperback the paradoxical and yet wholly appropriate and properly informative title *The Catholicity of Protestantism*. In the matter of form of presentation, if not of substantive doctrine, following his example, I have in my time published papers with such titles as "Do-gooders Doing No Good?" and "Is Pascal's Wager the Only Safe Bet?"

At the outset I should make one thing clear. When reports of my change of mind were spread by the media and the ubiquitous Internet, some commentators were quick to claim that my advanced age had something to do with my "conversion." It has been said that fear concentrates the mind powerfully, and these critics had concluded that expectations of an impending entrance into the afterlife had triggered a deathbed conversion. Clearly these people were familiar with neither my writings on the nonexistence of an afterlife nor with my current views on the topic. For over fifty years I have not simply denied the existence of God, but also the existence of an afterlife. My Gifford Lectures published as *The Logic of Mortality* represent the culmination of this process of thought. This is one area in which I have not changed my mind. Absent special revelation, a possibility that is well represented in this book by N. T. Wright's contribution, I do not think of myself "surviving" death. For the record, then, I want to lay to rest all those rumors that have me placing Pascalian bets.

I should point out, moreover, that this is not the first time I "changed my mind" on a fundamental issue. Among other things, readers who are familiar with my vigorous defense of free markets may be surprised to learn that I was once a Marxist (for details, see the second chapter of this book). In addition, over two decades ago I retracted my earlier view that all human choices are determined entirely by physical causes.

Since this is a book about why I changed my mind about the existence of God, an obvious question would be what I believed before the "change" and why. The first three chapters seek to answer this question, and the last seven chapters describe my discovery of the Divine. In the preparation of the last seven chapters, I was greatly helped by discussions with Professor Richard Swinburne and Professor Brian Leftow, the former and current occupants of the Nolloth Chair at Oxford.

There are two appendices to the book. The first is an analysis of the so-called new atheism of Richard Dawkins and others by Roy Abraham Varghese. The second is an open-ended dialogue on a topic of great interest to most religious believers—the issue of whether there is any kind of divine revelation in human history, with specific attention to the claims made about Jesus of Nazareth. In the interest of furthering the dialogue, the New Testament scholar N. T. Wright, who is the present bishop of Durham, kindly provided his assessment of the body of historical fact that underlies Christian theists' faith in Christ. In fact, I have to say here that Bishop Wright presents by far the best case for accepting Christian belief that I have ever seen.

Perhaps something should be said about my "notoriety" as an atheist, which is referenced in the subtitle. The first of my antitheological works was my 1950 paper "Theology and Falsification." That paper was later reprinted in *New Essays in Philosophical Theology* (1955), an anthology I coedited with Alasdair MacIntyre. *New Essays* was an attempt to gauge the impact on theological topics of what was then called the "revolution in philosophy." The next major work was *God and Philosophy*, first published in 1966 and reissued in 1975, 1984, and 2005. In his introduction to the 2005 edition, Paul Kurtz, one of the leading atheists of our age and author of the "Humanist Manifesto II," wrote that "Prometheus Books is delighted to present what by now has become a classic in the philosophy of religion." *God and Philosophy* was followed in 1976 by *The Presumption of Atheism*, which was published as *God, Freedom and Immortality* in the United States in 1984. Other relevant works were *Hume's Philosophy of Belief* and *Logic and Language* (first and second series), *An Introduction to Western Philosophy: Ideas and Arguments from Plato to Sartre*, *Darwinian Evolution*, and *The Logic of Mortality*.

It is paradoxical indeed that my first published argument for atheism was originally presented at a forum presided over by the greatest Christian apologist of the last century—the Socratic Club chaired by C. S. Lewis. Yet another paradox is the fact that my father was one of the leading Methodist writers and preachers in England. More-over, at the start of my career, I had no particular interest in becoming a professional philosopher.

Since, notoriously, all good things, if not all things without exception, must come to an end, I will end my introductory words here. I leave it to readers to decide what to make of my reasons for changing my mind on the question of God.

Antony Flew

PART I

MY DENIAL OF
THE DIVINE

I

THE CREATION
OF AN ATHEIST

I was not always an atheist. I began life quite religiously.
I was raised in a Christian home and attended a private
Christian school. In fact, I am the son of a preacher.

My father was a product of Merton College, Oxford,
and a minister of religion in the Wesleyan Methodist rather
than the established church, the Church of England.
Although his heart remained always in evangelism and,
as Anglicans would say, in parish work, my own earliest
memories of him are as tutor in New Testament studies at
the Methodist theological college in Cambridge. Later he
succeeded the head of that college and was to eventually
retire and die in Cambridge. In addition to the basic scholarly and teaching duties of these offices, my father undertook a great deal of work as a Methodist representative in
various interchurch organizations. He also served one-year
terms as president of both the Methodist Conference and
the Free Church Federal Council.

I would be hard-pressed to isolate or identify any signs in my boyhood of my later atheist convictions. In my youth, I attended Kingswood School in Bath, known informally as K.S. It was, and happily still remains, a public boarding school (an institution of a kind that everywhere else in the English-speaking world would be described, paradoxically, as a *private* boarding school). It had been founded by John Wesley, founder of the Methodist Church, for the education of the sons of his preachers. (A century or more after the foundation of Kingswood School, Queenswood School was founded in order to accommodate the daughters of Methodist preachers in the appropriately egalitarian way.)

I entered Kingswood as a committed and conscientious, if unenthusiastic, Christian. I could never see the point of worship and have always been far too unmusical to enjoy or even participate in hymn singing. I never approached any religious literature with the same unrestrained eagerness with which I consumed books on politics, history, science, or almost any other topic. Going to chapel or church, saying prayers, and all other religious practices were for me matters of more or less weary duty. Never did I feel the slightest desire to commune with God.

Why I should be—from my earliest memory—generally uninterested in the religious practices and issues that so shaped my father's world I cannot say. I simply don't recall feeling any interest or enthusiasm for such observances. Nor do I think I ever felt my mind enchanted or "my heart strangely warmed," to use Wesley's famous phrase, in Christian study or worship. Whether my youthful lack of enthusiasm for religion was a cause or effect—or both—who can say? But I can say that whatever faith I had when I entered K.S. was gone by the time I finished.

A THEORY OF DEVOLUTION

I am told that the Barna Group, a prominent Christian demographic polling organization, concluded from its surveys that in essence what you believe by the time you are thirteen is what you will die believing. Whether or not this finding is correct, I do know that the beliefs I formed in my early teenage years stayed with me for most of my adult life.

Just how and when the change began, I cannot remember precisely. But certainly, as with any thinking person, multiple factors combined in the creation of my convictions. Not the least among these factors was what Immanuel Kant called "an eagerness of mind not unbecoming to scholarship," which I believe I shared with my father. Both he and I were disposed to follow the path of "wisdom" as Kant described it: "It is wisdom that has the merit of selecting, from among innumerable problems that present themselves, those whose solution is important to humankind." My father's Christian convictions persuaded him that there could be nothing more "important to humankind" than the elucidation, propagation, and implementation of whatever is in truth the teaching of the New Testament. My intellectual journey took me in a different direction, of course, but one that was no less marked by the eagerness of mind I shared with him.

I also recall being most beneficially reminded by my father on more than one occasion that when biblical scholars want to become familiar with some peculiar Old Testament concept, they do not try to find an answer simply by thinking it through on their own. Instead, they collect and examine, with as much context as they can find, all available contemporary examples of the employment of the relevant Hebrew word. This scholarly approach in many ways formed the basis of my earliest intellectual explorations—and one I have yet to abandon—of collecting and examining, in context, all relevant information on a given subject. It is ironic, perhaps, that the household in which I grew up very likely instilled in me the enthusiasm for critical investigation that would eventually lead me to reject my father's faith.

THE FACE OF EVIL

I have said in some of my later atheist writings that I reached the conclusion about the nonexistence of God much too quickly, much too easily, and for what later seemed to me the wrong reasons. I reconsidered this negative conclusion at length and often, but for nearly seventy years thereafter I never found grounds sufficient to warrant any fundamental reversal. One of those early reasons for my conversion to atheism was the problem of evil.

My father took my mother and me on annual summer holidays abroad. Although these would not have been affordable on a minister's salary, they were made possible because my father often spent the early part of summer examining for the Higher School Certificate Examinations Board (now called A-level examinations) and had been paid for that work. We were also able to travel abroad cheaply since my father was fluent in German after two years of theological study in the University of Marburg before World War I. He was thus able to take us on holiday in Germany, and once or twice in France, without having to spend money on a travel agent. My father was also appointed to serve as the representative of Methodism at several international theological conferences. To these he took me, an only child, and my mother as nonparticipating guests.

I was greatly influenced by these early travels abroad during the years before World War II. I vividly recall the banners and signs outside small towns proclaiming, "Jews not wanted here." I remember signs outside the entrance to a public library proclaiming, "The regulations of this institution forbid the issuing of any books to Jewish bor-rowers." I observed a march of ten thousand brown-shirted storm troopers through a Bavarian summer night. Our fam-ily travels exposed me to squads of the Waffen-SS in their black uniforms with skull-and-crossbones caps.

Such experiences sketched the background of my youthful life and for me, as for many others, presented an inescapable challenge to the existence of an all-powerful God of love. The degree to which they influenced my think-ing I cannot measure. If nothing else, these experiences awoke in me a lifelong awareness of the twin evils of anti-Semitism and totalitarianism.

AN ENORMOUSLY LIVELY PLACE

To grow up during the 1930s and the 1940s in such a house-hold as ours—aligned as it was to the Methodist denomi-nation—was to be in Cambridge, but not of it. For a start, theology was not then and there accepted as the "queen of the sciences," as it had been in other institutions. Nor was a ministerial training college any sort of mainstream university. As a result, I never identified with Cambridge, although my father felt quite at home there. In any case, from 1936, when I started boarding school, I was almost never in Cambridge during term time.

Nevertheless, Kingswood was in my day an enormously lively place, presided over by a man who surely deserved to be rated one of the great headmasters. In the year before I arrived, it had won more open awards at Oxford and Cambridge than any other Headmasters' Conference school. Nor was our liveliness confined to the classroom and the laboratory.

No one should be surprised that, placed in this stirring environment, I began to question the firm faith of my fathers, a faith to which I had never felt any strong emotional attachment. By the time I was in the upper sixth form at K.S. (the lower sixth, incidentally, is equivalent to the eleventh grade in America and the upper sixth to the twelfth grade), I was regularly arguing with fellow sixth formers that the idea of a God who is both omnipotent and perfectly good is incompatible with the manifest evils and imperfections of the world. In my time at K.S., the regular Sunday sermon never contained any reference to a future life in either heaven or hell. When the headmaster, A. B. Sackett, was the preacher, which was infrequent, his message always concerned the wonders and glories of nature. At any rate, by the time I reached my fifteenth birthday, I rejected the thesis that the universe was created by an all-good, all-powerful God.

One might well ask if I never thought to consult my clergyman father about my doubts regarding the existence of God. I never did. For the sake of domestic peace and, in particular, in order to spare my father, I tried for as long as I could to conceal from everyone at home my irreligious conversion. I succeeded in this, as far as I know, for a good many years.

But by January 1946, when I was nearly twenty-three, the word had gotten out—and back to my parents—that I was both an atheist and a mortalist (a disbeliever in life after death) and that it was unlikely there would be any going back. So total and firm was my change, that it was thought futile to engage in any discussion on the matter at home. However, today, well over half a century later, I can say that my father would be hugely delighted by my present view on the existence of a God—not least because he would consider this a great help to the cause of the Christian church.

A DIFFERENT OXFORD

From Kingswood, I went on to Oxford University. I arrived at Oxford in the Hilary (January to March) term of 1942. World War II was in progress, and on one of my first days as an eighteen-year-old undergraduate, I was medically examined and then officially recruited into the Royal Air Force. During those wartime days, almost all physically fit male undergraduates spent one day of every term-time week in the appropriate service organization. In my case, this was the Oxford University Air Squadron.

This military service, which was part-time for one year and full-time thereafter, was entirely noncombatant. It involved learning some Japanese at the School of Oriental and African Studies at London University and thereafter translating intercepted and deciphered Japanese army air force signals at Bletchley Park. After Japan surrendered (and while awaiting my turn for demobilization), I worked at translating intercepted signals from the newly constructed French army of occupation in what was then West Germany.

When I returned to full-time studies at the University of Oxford early in January 1946 and was due to take my final examination in the summer of 1947, the Oxford to which I returned was a very different place. It seemed a much more exciting institution than the one I had left nearly three years earlier. There was also a greater variety of both peacetime careers and actual military careers now safely completed than there had been after World War I. I was myself reading for a degree in the final Honors School of Literae Humaniores, and some of my lectures on the history of classical Greece were given by veterans who had been active in assisting the Greek resistance either in Crete or on the Greek mainland, making the lectures more romantic and stimulating to an undergraduate audience.

I took my final examinations in the summer term of
1947. To my surprise and delight, I was awarded a First
(the U.K. expression for passing your undergraduate examinations with first-class honors). On receiving this, I went
back to John Mabbott, my personal tutor at St. John's College. I told him that I had abandoned my previous goal
of working for a second undergraduate degree in the then
newly established School of Philosophy and Psychology. I
now intended to start working for a higher degree in philosophy.

WAXING PHILOSOPHIC

Mabbott arranged for me to engage in postgraduate philosophical studies under the supervision of Gilbert Ryle, who
was then the Waynflete Professor of Metaphysical Philosophy at the University of Oxford. Ryle, in the second term
of the academic year 1947–48, was the senior of Oxford's
three philosophy chairs.

It was only many years later that I learned from Mabbott's captivating book *Oxford Memories* that Mabbott and
Ryle had been friends since they first met at Oxford. Had I
been at a different college and had I been asked by a different college tutor which of the three possible professional
supervisors I would have preferred, I would certainly have

chosen Henry Price, because of our shared interest in what is now known as parapsychology but was then still called psychical research. As it was, my first book was entitled *A New Approach to Psychical Research,* and Price and I became speakers at conferences concerned with psychical research. But I am sure I would not have won the university prize in philosophy in an exceptionally strong year, had my graduate studies been supervised by Henry Price. We would have spent too much of our time talking about our common interests.

After devoting the academic year 1948 to reading for a higher degree in philosophy under Ryle's supervision, I won the aforementioned university prize, the John Locke Scholarship in Mental Philosophy. I was then appointed to what in any other Oxford college but Christ Church would have been called a (probationary) fellowship—that is to say, a full-time teaching job. In the vocabulary of Christ Church, however, I was said to have become a (probationary) student.

During the year I taught at Oxford, the teachings of the noted philosopher Ludwig Wittgenstein, whose approach to philosophy would influence my own, entered Oxford. However, these teachings, later published as his *Blue Book, Brown Book,* and *Lectures on Mathematics,* came in the form of typescripts of single lectures—and they were accompanied by letters from Wittgenstein indicating to whom the particular lectures might or might not be shown. A colleague and I contrived to produce, without breaking any promise to Wittgenstein, copies of all the Wittgenstein lectures then available in Oxford, so that anyone who wished could read these lectures.

This good end—I write here in the vocabulary of the moral philosophers of that period—was attained by first asking everyone we knew to be actively philosophizing at Oxford at that time whether they possessed any typescripts of Wittgenstein lectures, and if so, which ones. Then, since that was long before photocopiers, we found and hired a typist to produce enough copies to satisfy the demand. (Little did we know that circulating these seminal typescripts only to members of an in-group and then only under vows of secrecy would provoke outsiders to comment that Wittgenstein, who was undoubtedly a philosopher of genius, often behaved like a charlatan pretending to be man of genius!)

Ryle had gotten to know Wittgenstein when the Austrian philosopher had visited Cambridge. Subsequently, Ryle developed a friendship with him, persuading Wittgenstein to join him on a walking tour in the English Lake District in 1930 or 1931. Ryle never published any account of this tour or of what during it he had learned from and about Wittgenstein. But after that tour, and ever after, Ryle acted as a mediator between Wittgenstein and what philosophers call "the external world."

How necessary that mediation sometimes was may be revealed by the record of a conversation between Wittgenstein, who was Jewish, and his sisters immediately after Hitler's soldiers had seized control of Austria. Wittgenstein assured his sisters that, because of their close connections with the "main people and families" of the former regime, neither he nor they were in any danger. When later I became a professional teacher of philosophy, I was reluctant to reveal to my pupils that Wittgenstein, whom I and many of my colleagues considered to be a philosophical genius, had been so deluded in practical matters.

I personally witnessed Wittgenstein in action at least once. This was during my time as an undergraduate when Wittgenstein visited the Jowett Society. His announced subject was *"Cogito ergo sum,"* derived, of course, from the French philosopher René Descartes's famous statement "I think therefore I am." The room was packed. The audience hung on to every one of the great man's words. But the only thing I can now remember about his comments is that they had absolutely no discernible connection with the announced topic. So when Wittgenstein had finished, Emeritus Professor H. A. Prichard got up. With evident exasperation, he asked what "Herr Wittgenstein"— the Cambridge Ph.D. was apparently not recognized at Oxford!—"thought about *Cogito ergo sum.*" Wittgenstein responded by pointing at his forehead with the index finger of his right hand and saying only, "*Cogito ergo sum*. That's a very peculiar sentence." I thought then, and still do, that the most suitable riposte to Wittgenstein's statement would have been an adaptation of one of the cartoon captions in James Thurber's *Men, Women and Dogs*: "Maybe you don't have charm, Lily, but you're enigmatic."

LOCKING HORNS WITH LEWIS

During my time as a graduate student supervised by Gilbert Ryle, I became aware that it was his obviously principled practice always to respond directly, person to person, to any objection made to any of his philosophical contentions. My own conjecture, although Ryle certainly never revealed this to me or, as far as I know, to anyone else, is that he was obeying the command that Plato in the *Republic* attributes to Socrates: "We must follow the argument wherever it leads." Among other things, this principle requires that every objection made person to person must also be met person to person. It is a principle I myself have tried to follow throughout a long and very widely controversial life.

This Socratic principle also formed the inspiration of the Socratic Club, a group that was really at the center of what intellectual life there was in wartime Oxford. The Socratic Club was a lively forum for debates between atheists and Christians, and I was a regular participant at its meetings. Its redoubtable president from 1942 to 1954 was the famous Christian writer C. S. Lewis. The club convened every Monday evening during term time in the underground Junior Common Room of St. Hilda's College. In his preface to the first issue of the *Socratic Digest*, Lewis cited Socrates' exhortation to "follow the argument wherever it leads." He noted that this "arena specially devoted to the conflict between Christian and unbeliever was a novelty."

Many of the leading atheists at Oxford locked horns with Lewis and his fellow Christians. By far the best-known encounter was the celebrated February 1948 debate between Lewis and Elizabeth Anscombe, which led Lewis to revise the third chapter of his book *Miracles*. I still remember being a member of a small group of friends returning together from that great debate, walking directly behind Elizabeth Anscombe and her party. She was exultant, and her friends were equally exultant. Immediately in front of this party, C. S. Lewis trod alone, walking as rapidly as he could to refuge in his rooms in Magdalen College, just off the bridge we were all crossing.

Although many have characterized Lewis as permanently demoralized by the outcome of this debate, Anscombe herself thought differently. "The meeting of the Socratic Club at which I read my paper," she wrote later, "has been described by several of his friends as a horrible and shocking experience which upset him very much. Neither Dr. Havard (who had Lewis and me to dinner a few weeks later) nor Professor Jack Bennett remembered any such feelings on Lewis' part.... I am inclined to construe the odd accounts of the matter by some of his friends ... as an interesting example of the phenomenon called 'projection.'"[1]

Lewis was the most effective Christian apologist for certainly the latter part of the twentieth century. When the BBC recently asked if I had absolutely refuted Lewis's Christian apologetic, I replied: "No. I just didn't believe there was sufficient reason for believing it. But of course when I later came to think about theological things, it seemed to me that the case for the Christian revelation is a very strong one, if you believe in any revelation at all."

HIGHLY POSITIVE DEVELOPMENTS

During my last term at the University of Oxford, the publication of A. J. Ayer's book *Language, Truth and Logic* had persuaded many members of the Socratic Club that the Ayerian heresy of logical positivism—the contention that all religious propositions are without cognitive significance—had to be refuted. The first and only paper I ever read to the Socratic Club, "Theology and Falsification," provided what I then considered to be a sufficient refutation. I believed I had achieved a total victory and there was no room for further debate.

It was also at Oxford that I met Annis Donnison, my wife-to-be. We were introduced by Annis's sister-in-law to be at a Labor Club social at Oxford. After that introduction to Annis, I paid no attention to anyone else at that social. The occasion at the end of that social when I made arrangements with Annis for our next meeting constituted the first occasion in which I had ever dated a girl. Our social conditions at the time of our first meeting were very different. I was *teaching* at Christ Church, a men-only institution, whereas Annis was in her first year as a *pupil* at Somerville, a women's college, which, like all the other women's colleges in Oxford at that time and for a decade or so thereafter, simply expelled any student who "committed marriage."

My future mother-in-law was understandably concerned about an academically senior person like me dating her much younger daughter. She therefore consulted her son, my future brother-in-law. He assured her that I was, as she would have put it herself, "in love or something" and would be brokenhearted if I were to be prevented from continuing that dating relationship. I have always assumed that he simply wanted his younger sister to be left alone to conduct her own life, knowing her to be a sensible girl who could be trusted not to make any hasty decisions.

Though I had long since departed from my father's faith, I nonetheless reflected what I had been taught by my Methodist parents; I never even attempted to seduce Annis before our wedding, believing that such behavior is always morally wrong. Nor, as the son of an academic, did I entertain thought of persuading Annis to marry me before she had graduated and won her degree.

I officially ceased to be an untenured tutor at Christ Church, Oxford, at the end of September 1950 and began to serve as a lecturer in moral philosophy at the University of Aberdeen in Scotland on October 1 that year.

BEYOND OXFORD

During my years in Aberdeen, I gave several radio talks, participated in three or four radio discussions sponsored by the then newly founded and militantly highbrow BBC Third Programme, and served as a subject in several psychological experiments. For us the great attractions of Aberdeen were the friendliness of almost everyone we met; the strength and variety of the adult education movement; the very fact that Aberdeen was a city in Scotland rather than in England, which was new to us; and the fact that it gave us such varied possibilities for walking along the coast and in the Cairngorms. I don't think we ever failed to join the Cairngorm Club on one of its regular monthly trips to those hills.

During the summer of 1954, I traveled from Aberdeen, by way of North America, to become professor of philosophy at the University College of North Staffordshire, which later earned its charter as the University of Keele. Throughout the seventeen years I spent there, Keele remained the nearest thing the United Kingdom has ever had to such U.S. liberal arts colleges as Oberlin and Swarthmore. I quickly became devoted to it and left only when it began, slowly but irresistibly, to lose its distinctiveness.

Having spent the academic year 1970–71 as a visiting professor in the United States, I resigned at the end of 1971 from what had by then become the University of Keele (my successor at Keele was Richard Swinburne). In January 1972 I moved to the University of Calgary in Alberta, Canada. My initial intention was to settle there. However, in May 1973, after only three semesters in Calgary, I transferred to the University of Reading, where I remained until the end of 1982.

Before requesting and receiving early retirement from Reading, I had contracted to teach for one semester each year at York University, Toronto, during the remaining six years of my normal academic life. Halfway through that period, however, I resigned from York University in order to accept an invitation from the Social Philosophy and Policy

Center at Bowling Green State University, in Ohio, to serve the next three years as a Distinguished Research Fellow. The invitation was next extended for another three years. After that, I finally and fully retired to—and still reside in—Reading.

This outline of my career does not address the question of why I became a philosopher. Given my philosophical interests at Kingswood, it may seem that I was all set to become a professional philosopher long before going up to Oxford. In fact, I scarcely knew there existed such a creature at the time. Even in my two terms at Oxford before joining the RAF, the nearest I came to philosophy was at meetings of the Socratic Club. My main interests outside my studies were political. That was still true after January 1946, when the subjects I studied began to include philosophy.

I only began to see a career in philosophy as a remote possibility a few months before taking finals in December 1947. Had my fears of being placed in Class II been realized, I would have read for a second set of finals, with a concentration on psychology, in the new School of Philosophy, Psychology, and Physiology. Instead, I went straight to work for the similarly new-fangled B.Phil. under the supervision of Gilbert Ryle. It was only in the last weeks of 1949, after being appointed to a probationary studentship at Christ Church, that I set my course (and indeed, burned my bridges) by refusing an offer to join the Administrative

Class of the Home Civil Service—a choice I regretted until I received the offer from Aberdeen.

In the next two chapters, I try to detail the case I built over the years against the existence of God. I delve first into a half century of atheist arguments I assembled and developed and then proceed, in Chapter 3, to trace the various twists and turns my philosophy took, particularly as it can be charted through my frequent debates on the subject of atheism.

Through it all, I hope it will be seen, as I have said in the past, that my long-standing interest in religion was never anything other than prudential, moral, or simply curious. I say prudential since, if there is a God or gods who involve themselves in human affairs, it would be madly imprudent not to try as far as possible to keep on the right side of them. I say my interest has been moral, since I should be glad to find what Matthew Arnold once called "the eternal *not for ourselves* that makes for righteousness." And I say my interest has been curious, since any scientifically minded person must want to discover what, if anything, it is possible to know about these matters. Even so, it may well be that no one is as surprised as I am that my exploration of the Divine has after all these years turned from denial to discovery.

2

WHERE THE
EVIDENCE LEADS

When Alice journeyed through the looking glass in Lewis Carroll's famous fantasy, she met a queen who claimed to be "one hundred and one, five months and a day":

"I can't believe *that*!" said Alice.

"Can't you?" the Queen said in a pitying tone. "Try again: draw a long breath, and shut your eyes."

Alice laughed. "There's no use trying," she said: "one *can't* believe impossible things."

"I daresay you haven't had much practice," said the Queen. "When I was your age, I always did it for half-an-hour a day. Why, sometimes I've believed as many as six impossible things before breakfast."

I daresay I must sympathize with Alice. Had I tried to imagine the path my life and study has taken—even after

I commenced studies in philosophy under the supervision of Gilbert Ryle—I must certainly have dismissed it all as improbable, if not impossible.

I could hardly have imagined, when I first published "Theology and Falsification," that within the next half century I would publish some thirty-five volumes on a wide variety of philosophical topics. Though I am most known for my writings on the question of God's existence, this was by no means my only area of interest. Over the years, I have written on themes ranging from linguistic philosophy to logic; from moral, social, and political philosophy to the philosophy of science; and from parapsychology and education to the free will–determinism debate and the idea of the afterlife.

But though I became an atheist at the age of fifteen and also developed various other philosophical or semiphilosophical interests while a student at Kingswood School, it took years for my philosophical views to mature and solidify. By the time they did so, I had arrived at the guiding principles that would not only govern my lifetime of writing and reasoning, but also eventually dictate a dramatic turn: from atheism to theism.

EARLY EXPLORATIONS … AND EMBARRASSMENTS

Some of my philosophical views had taken shape even before my arrival at Kingswood School. I was already a professing Communist on my enrollment there, and I remained a hotly energetic left-wing socialist until the early 1950s, when I resigned from the Labor Party, Britain's historically leftist movement.

What prevented me from actually joining the Communist Party, as several of my Kingswood contemporaries did, was the behavior of the British Communist Party after the German-Soviet Pact of 1939 (when I was still a teenager). In obedience to instructions from Moscow, this servile and treacherous organization started to denounce the war against National Socialist (Nazi) Germany as "imperialist" and hence no business of the British people. These denunciations continued even through 1940, while the country was threatened with invasion. However, this so-called imperialist war suddenly became a "progressive, people's war" (from the Communists' perspective) when German forces invaded the USSR. In subsequent years, I became increasingly critical of the theory and practice of Communism, with its thesis that history is driven by laws akin to those of the physical sciences.

During this period, like many of my contemporaries at Kingswood, I discovered the expository writings of C. E. M. Joad. At that time, Joad was the philosopher best known to the British public because of his broadcast discussions on philosophical topics and his popular writing style (he authored some seventy-five books in all). Partly through reading Joad I discovered various best-selling but, as I have since learned, lamentably unreliable books about psychical research, the subject now more usually known as parapsychology.

I suppose many of us, as we age, look back on our youth with a mixture of nostalgia and embarrassment. I'm sure these emotions are quite common. However, not all of us have the added misfortune of having recorded—and published, no less—some of those embarrassments. But such is my case.

My interest in parapsychology led to the 1953 publication of my first, excruciatingly ill-written book. I had written and delivered a pair of broadcast talks in 1951 attacking popular misrepresentations of alleged parapsychological phenomena. These talks prompted the invitation from a publisher to write a book on the subject, which, in the brash arrogance of youth, I entitled *A New Approach to Psychical Research*.

The book treated both the alleged facts and the philosophical problems of parapsychology. I hope I may be forgiven some of the stylistic defects in that work, since those are partly due to the fact that the publishers wanted it written in the style of a frivolous essay. There were, however, more substantial faults. On the empirical side, I accepted the since discredited experimental work of S. G. Soal, a London University mathematician and researcher. On the philosophical side, I had not yet grasped the full significance for parapsychology of the sort of argument sketched by the Scottish philosopher David Hume in Section X of his first *Inquiry*. Decades later, I compiled a book of readings, which I consider more satisfactory than any previously available on the subject, entitled *Readings in the Philosophical Problems of Parapsychology*. In my editorial contributions I summed up what, in the intervening years, I had learned of the solutions to those problems.

EXPLORING NEW INTERESTS

Two other philosophical interests arose from popular scientific writings I read in my youth. The first was in the suggestion that evolutionary biology could provide a guarantee of progress. This suggestion was powerfully made in one of Julian Huxley's early pieces in *Essays of a Biologist*. He pursued it, with increasing desperation, for the rest of his life. In *Time, the Refreshing River* and in *History Is on Our Side,* Joseph Needham combined this suggestion with a Marxist philosophy of history, a doctrine asserting natural laws of inexorable historical development. Thus Marxists believed that there are universal laws, such as the inevitability of class warfare, governing the development of societies. It was partly in order to refute this literature that, when I was asked in the mid-1960s to contribute to the series New

Studies in Ethics, I undertook to produce a book-length essay, *Evolutionary Ethics*. (This was also partly the reason I wrote *Darwinian Evolution* when I was asked to contribute to a series on movements and ideas in the early 1980s. In this latter book, I sought to show that the prestige of Darwinism has been invoked to sustain other ideas and beliefs that lack any solid foundation—such as the idea that Darwin's theory is a guarantee of human progress.)

The second philosophical interest aroused by my reading of popular scientific literature was in attempts to draw neo-Berkeleyan conclusions from twentieth-century developments in physics. Neo-Berkeleyans belong to the school of philosophy called idealism. Idealists believe that all of physical reality is purely mental, and that only minds and the contents of minds exist. The main source books here were the works of Sir James Jeans and Sir Arthur Eddington. It was Susan Stebbing, with her *Philosophy and the Physicists*, who taught me how to begin cutting my way out of this particular jungle.

Years later, in *An Introduction to Western Philosophy*, I would try to show that such idealism was fatal for science. I cited a passage from *Mind, Perception and Science* by a distinguished British neurologist, the aptly named Lord Brain (W. Russell Brain), who noted that neurologists are usually idealists who believe that the act of perceiving an object is simply an event in the subject's brain.

I also quoted Bertrand Russell's claim that "perception gives no immediate knowledge of a physical object." If this were true, I said, then there is no such thing as perception. And since the scientists do and must rely for the ultimate vindication of their discoveries upon direct observation, this conclusion necessarily undermines the findings from which it is derived. In short, this view removes the bases of all scientific inference. Against this I argued that in normal conscious perception I must have an appropriate sensory experience (e.g., the sound and sight of a hammer driving in a nail); and that, if anything is truly said to have been perceived, then that thing (the hammer and the nail) must have been part of the cause of my having that experience.

NEW INSIGHTS IN PHILOSOPHY

During my time at Oxford (1946–50), a new way of doing philosophy, sometimes called the "revolution in philosophy," was in full bloom. While at Oxford (for two years as an undergraduate, another as a postgraduate, and eighteen months as a junior tutor at Christ Church), I saturated myself in this "new philosophy," which its many enemies described as "linguistic" or "ordinary language." The dominant philosophical figures at Oxford at the time were Gilbert Ryle and John Austin. Ryle, as I have noted, was supervisor of my B.Phil. studies. I saw more of Austin when, after my appointment at Christ Church, I was able to become a regular attender at his now famous "Saturday mornings"—discussions held in his Oxford rooms on Saturday mornings to discuss the progress of science.

This Oxford philosophy of the 1940s and the 1950s provided several valuable insights that I still hold to be true. Perhaps the most important and wide-ranging of these insights was that we must become constantly and crisply conscious of how all philosophy (insofar as philosophy is a conceptual inquiry) must be concerned with correct verbal usage. We can have no access to concepts except through study of linguistic usage and, hence, the use of those words through which these concepts are expressed. This insight recalled to me the biblical scholars I mentioned earlier (exemplified by my father) who study some peculiar Old Testament concept by collecting and examining, with as much context as they can find, all available usages of the relevant Hebrew word.

As heady and as influential on the development of my own philosophical direction as those days were, this "new philosophy" was neither so new nor so necessarily narrow as it sometimes appeared. The "revolution" involved a focus on conceptual grammar, the use of concepts in ordinary language, a study that would help eliminate many of the apparent problems in philosophy. One such problem was whether we could have knowledge by acquaintance of the "external" (logically public) world. This problem was first formulated in the seventeenth century by Descartes and later accepted without question by most of his greatest successors—Locke, Berkeley, Hume, and Kant among them. This "new philosophy," however, rejected this problem of Cartesian skepticism by rejecting its starting point: that a person was an incorporeal subject who had only private experience. This belief was inconsistent with the assumption in our regular speech that we know by acquaintance both the physical world and other people. But as I said, this was not completely new; the Plato who wrote *Theaetetus* and the Aristotle of the *Nicomachean Ethics* would have been entirely at home in seminars run by Ryle and Austin.

PROGRESS IN PHILOSOPHY

Before leaving Oxford, I delivered materials for the collection entitled *Logic and Language,* Series 1, to the publisher. A second series soon followed. Both volumes were edited with a short introduction by me, the first in 1951 and the second in 1953. So, soon after taking my position as lecturer at the University of Aberdeen, I found myself acting as the unappointed but nevertheless recognized spokesman in Scotland for "Oxford linguistic philosophy." When the

Scots Philosophy Club, a collection of all those teaching philosophy in Scotland, launched a new journal, *The Philosophical Quarterly*, an early issue contained an attack on this Oxford school. To this the editor asked me to respond. The result, "Philosophy and Language," later became, in a modified form, the introductory chapter in a third collection of papers titled *Essays in Conceptual Analysis*. A critic from the English side, Michael Dummett, described the movement as "the cult of ordinary language" and curiously claimed that "membership" in this school "apparently depends upon nomination by Professor Flew."[1]

Certainly some of the practitioners of the new philosophy, even if only very few, were devoted to trivial, esoteric, and pointless inquiries. I reacted against such apparent triviality and pointlessness with a paper I wrote and read to the B.Phil. Club entitled "Matter That Matters." I argued that it was both possible and desirable to concentrate on problems that even philosophically uninstructed laypersons could perceive as interesting and important, instead of wasting time and effort in philosophical shadowboxing (and this I said without abandoning—indeed, while positively profiting from—insights obtained at Oxford).

I came to see, as I would write in *An Introduction to Western Philosophy*, that there can be progress in philosophy despite the general absence of consensus. The lack of consensus in philosophy is not an independently suffi-

cient demonstration that the subject does not make progress. The attempt to show that there is no philosophical
knowledge by simply urging that there is always someone
who can be relied on to remain unconvinced is a common fallacy made even by a distinguished philosopher like
Bertrand Russell. I called it the But-there-is-always-some-
one-who-will-never-agree Diversion. Then there is the
charge that in philosophy it is never possible to prove to
someone that you are right and he or she is wrong. But the
missing piece in this argument is the distinction between
producing a proof and persuading a person. A person can
be persuaded by an abominable argument and remain
unconvinced by one that ought to be accepted.

Progress in philosophy is different from progress in
science, but that does not mean it is therefore impossible. In philosophy you spotlight the essential nature of
deductive argument; you distinguish between questions
about the validity or invalidity of arguments and questions about the truth or falsity of their premises or conclusion; you indicate the strict usage of the term *fallacy*;
and you identify and elucidate such fallacies as the But-
there-is-always-someone-who-will-never-agree Diversion.
To the extent that these things are accomplished with better reasoning and greater effectiveness, progress will be
seen—even as consensus and persuasion remain elusive
and incomplete.

PAYING MORE ATTENTION TO ATHEISM

C. S. Lewis's Socratic Club was open for business during the heyday of the new philosophy, and the Socratic principle I saw exemplified there—of following the evidence wherever it may lead—increasingly became a guiding principle in the development, refinement, and sometimes reversal of my own philosophical views. It was also in meetings of the Socratic Club that the "linguistic" philosophers, who were accused of trivializing a once profound discipline, began to explore what Kant famously distinguished as the three great questions of philosophy—God, freedom, and immortality. My contribution to the discussions in this forum was a paper entitled "Theology and Falsification."

As I have mentioned, the grounds on which I embraced atheism at the age of fifteen were clearly inadequate. They were built on what I later described as two "juvenile insistencies": (1) the problem of evil was a decisive disproof of the existence of an all-good, all-powerful God; and (2) the "free-will defense" did not relieve the Creator of responsibility for the manifest ills of creation. But since my schooldays I had devoted much more attention to the reasons for or against reaching atheist conclusions. My opening shot in this investigation was "Theology and Falsification."

"Theology and Falsification" was first presented in the summer of 1950 to the Socratic Club at Oxford and then published in October in an ephemeral undergraduate journal called *University*. The first reprinting appeared in 1955 in *New Essays in Philosophical Theology,* a collection jointly edited by Alasdair MacIntyre and myself. *New Essays* was a substantial collection of contributions to the philosophy of religion from the perspective of the new philosophy. The *Times Literary Supplement* at the time described it as "possessing a certain virginal freshness."

My main objective in "Theology and Falsification" was to clarify the nature of the claims made by religious believers. I asked: Do the numerous qualifications surrounding theological utterances result in their dying the death by a thousand qualifications? If you make a claim, it is meaningful only if it excludes certain things. For instance, the claim that the earth is a globe excludes the possibility that it is flat. And although it may appear flat, this apparent contradiction can be explained by the earth's great size, the perspective from which we are viewing it, and so on. So, once you add appropriate qualifications, the claim can be satisfactorily reconciled with phenomena that appear to contradict it. But if contradictory phenomena and associated qualifications keep multiplying, then the claim itself becomes suspect.

If we say that God loves us, then we must ask what phenomena the claim excludes. Obviously, the existence of pain and suffering emerge as problems for such a claim.

Theists tell us that, with appropriate qualifications, these phenomena can be reconciled with the existence and love of God. But then the question arises as to why we should not simply conclude that God does not love us. Theists, it would seem, do not let any phenomena count against the claim that God loves us. This would mean that nothing counts for it either. It effectively becomes empty. I concluded that "a fine, brash hypothesis may thus be killed by inches, the death by a thousand qualifications."

Although my intention in raising these questions seems clear, I have repeatedly encountered claims that I was expounding my views about the meaning—or more often the *meaninglessness*—of all religious language. Just as prevalent have been claims that I was explicitly appealing to (or at least taking for granted) and relying upon the notorious verification principle of the old original Vienna Circle of logical positivists—that only statements that could be verified using the methods of the sciences were meaningful.

But in fact I have never maintained any comprehensive thesis about the meaning *or* the meaninglessness of all religious language. My primary purpose in "Theology and Falsification" was to spice up the bland dialogue between logical positivism and the Christian religion and to set discussion between belief and unbelief upon different and more fruitful lines. I was not offering any comprehensive doctrine about all religious belief or all religious language. I was not saying that statements of religious belief were meaningless. I simply challenged religious believers to explain how their statements are to be understood, especially in the light of conflicting data.

LEARNING FROM DISAGREEMENT

The paper elicited numerous responses, some of which appeared decades later and many of which helped me to sharpen—and, at times, correct—my views. Perhaps the most radical response was the first, from R. M. Hare, who would later hold the post of White's Professor of Moral Philosophy at Oxford. Hare suggested that religious utterances should be interpreted not as the making of statements, but as expressions of what he called a blik—something like a general approach or a general attitude. A blik, as he described it, is simply an interpretation of our experience that cannot be verified or falsified. As far as I know, Hare has never developed this idea further in print, but it is not one that would please religious believers, since it denied any rational basis to belief.

In the original discussion, Basil Mitchell, who succeeded C. S. Lewis as president of the Socratic Club, said that there was something odd about my presentation of the theologians' case. Theological utterances must be assertions, and to be assertions there must be something that would count against their truth. He pointed out that theologians do not deny this and, in fact, the theological problem of evil arose precisely because the existence of pain seems to count against the truth that God loves humankind. Their response has been the free-will defense. But Mitchell admitted that believers are often in danger of converting their assertions into formulas that are empty of meaning.

In Mitchell's *Faith and Logic,* I. M. Crombie, a philosopher known for his work on Plato, presented a much more thorough treatment of the topic. Theists believe in a mystery beyond experience, Crombie said, but he claims to detect traces of this mystery in experience. Furthermore, theists contend that to express their belief they are obliged to use language governed by paradoxical rules.[2]

Crombie noted that you can understand theological statements only if you do justice to three propositions: theists believe God is a transcendent being and statements about God apply to God and not to the world; theists believe God is transcendent and therefore beyond comprehension; since God is a mystery and since to gain attention we have to talk intelligibly, we can only talk about God in images. Theological statements are human images of divine truths that can be expressed as parables.[3]

Other respondents to "Theology and Falsification" included Raeburne Heimbeck and the Anglican divine Eric Mascall. In his *Theology and Meaning*, Heimbeck, Central Washington University professor emeritus of philosophy and religious studies, charged that "Theology and Falsification" made three important mistakes. First, it assumed that the meaning of any sentence is the same as the empirical implications of what it asserts. Second, it wrongly implied that counting against a belief is the same as being incompatible with it. Finally, it assumed that statements about God that express the love or existence of God are in principle unfalsifiable. The fundamental error, in his view, was that of identifying the grounds for believing a statement to be true or false with the conditions that would make it true or false.[4] Mascall took a page from the Wittgensteinians by pointing out that we can discover if a statement is meaningful only by determining if people can understand it in the linguistic context and community in which it is used.[5]

I have cited these responses at some length partially to illustrate the role of "Theology and Falsification" in stimulating new ripples of thought that helped stir up the stagnant pool of theological discourse. This discussion continues to the present day. In fact, the spring 2005 issue of the *Richmond Journal of Philosophy* featured yet another article discussing the merits of my arguments from 1950.

I also mention the responses to "Theology and Falsification" because the debate it engendered has had an effect on me and my philosophical views. How could it fail to do so, if I am consistent in my intention to follow the evidence wherever it leads? Indeed, in the silver jubilee reprint of the paper, I conceded the validity of two charges made by critics. Basil Mitchell had taken me to task for an oddity on my conduct of the theologians' case. Mitchell demonstrated that theologians do not deny that the fact of pain counts against the assertion that God loves humankind, and it is precisely this that generates the theological problem of evil. I think he is right in this. I also acknowledged the force of Heimbeck's critique and said I was wrong to collapse the distinction between "counts against" and "is incompatible with." My main argument bore directly only on the latter.

GOD AND PHILOSOPHY

Eleven years after *New Essays,* I published *God and Philosophy.* This was an attempt to present and examine the case for Christian theism. I could not find any previous presentation of the case that was widely accepted by contemporary believers as either adequate or standard. I tried asking Christian friends and colleagues for suggestions, but I found that there was little or no overlap between the resulting lists they offered. So I assembled from several sources the strongest case I could, urging those who were dissatisfied to buckle to and produce something they and their cobelievers might find more satisfactory.

God and Philosophy was first published in 1966. The book was reissued in 1984 as *God: A Critical Enquiry.* A final edition, with a publisher's foreword and a new and very unsatisfactory introduction by myself, was released by Prometheus in 2005.

In *God and Philosophy* I propounded a systematic argument for atheism. At the outset, I contended that our starting point should be the question of the consistency, applicability, and legitimacy of the very concept of God. In the succeeding chapters I addressed both the arguments of natural theology and the claims of divine revelation, while analyzing the notions of explanation, order, and purpose. Drawing on David Hume and other like-minded thinkers, I argued that the design, cosmological, and moral arguments for God's existence are invalid. I also tried to show that it was impossible validly to infer from a particular religious experience that it had as its object a transcendent divine being.

But the most significant contribution of the volume was the chapter "Beginning from the Beginning." I noted that three issues in particular must be answered with respect to the concept of God:

How God is to be identified.

How positive as opposed to negative terms like *incorporeal* can be applied to God.

How the inconsistency of defined characteristics of God with undenied facts can be explained (i.e., how the ills in the universe are to be reconciled with the existence of an omnipotent God).

The second and third of these questions had been defended by theists with the theory of analogy when talking of God's attributes and with the free-will defense when dealing with the problem of evil. But it was the first question that had never before been sufficiently highlighted.

Identification and individuation are matters of picking out an agreed-upon, recognized, and constant subject of discourse. But it was far from obvious how such a singular substance as the Mosaic God could be identified as separable and separate from the whole "created" universe. And what sense, if any, can be given to the insistence that this Being persists always one and the same, yet is active either through time or—still more perplexing—somehow "outside" time? Until and unless we have a genuine, coherent, and applicable concept, the question of whether such a being exists cannot properly arise. In other words, we cannot begin to discuss reasons for believing that a specific sort of God exists until we establish how to identify the God we mean to discuss. Much less can we understand how that same individual might be reidentified through the passage of time. So, for instance, how could "a person without a body (i.e., a spirit) who is present everywhere" be identified and reidentified—and thus qualify as a possible subject for various descriptions?

Theists responded to this line of thought in several ways. Most notable of all was Richard Swinburne (my successor at the University of Keele and later the Nolloth Professor of the Philosophy of the Christian Religion at Oxford) with his book *The Coherence of Theism.* He reasoned that the fact that the only O's we have ever seen are X does not imply that it is not coherent to suppose that there are O's that are not X. He said that no one has any business arguing that, just because all the so-and-so's with which they happen themselves to have been acquainted were such and such, therefore such-and-suchness must be an essential characteristic of anything that is to be properly rated a so-and-so. About identity, he argued that the identity of a person is something ultimate and cannot be analyzed in terms of continuity of body, memory, or character. J. L. Mackie, an atheist philosopher, accepted Swinburne's definition of God as a spirit who is everywhere present, all-powerful, and all-knowing and simply asserted that "there is really no problem" when it comes to identification and individuation.[6]

A historian of philosophy, Frederick Copleston, acknowledged the force of the problem I raised regarding the coherence of the concept of God and responded with a different kind of answer. "I do not think," he said, "that it can be justifiably demanded of the human mind that it should be able to pin down God like a butterfly in a showcase." According to him:

> God becomes a reality for the human mind in the personal movement of transcendence. In this movement, God appears as the unseen goal of the movement. And inasmuch as the Transcendent cannot be grasped in itself and overflows, so to speak, our conceptual web, doubt inevitably tends to arise. But, within the movement of transcendence, doubt is at once counterbalanced by the affirmation involved in the movement itself. It is within the context of this personal movement of the human spirit that God becomes a reality for man.[7]

What do I think today about the arguments laid out in *God and Philosophy*? In a 2004 letter to *Philosophy Now*, I observed that I now consider *God and Philosophy* to be a historical relic (but, of course, one cannot follow the evidence where it leads without giving others the chance to show you new perspectives you had not fully considered). And my current views on the themes treated there are presented in Part II of this book, "My Discovery of the Divine."

THE PRESUMPTION OF ATHEISM

A decade after *God and Philosophy,* I produced *The Presumption of Atheism* (published as *God, Freedom and Immortality* in the United States). In this book, I argued that a discussion about God's existence should start with the presumption of atheism, that the onus of proof must lie with the theists. I pointed out that this new approach puts the whole question of the existence of God into an entirely fresh perspective. It helps smoke out conceptual problems with theism that might otherwise escape attention and forces theists to begin from the absolute beginning. Theists' use of the word *God* must be provided with a meaning that makes it theoretically possible for an actual being to be so described. Consequently, I maintained, with this fresh perspective the whole enterprise of theism appears even more precarious than it did before.

The presumption of atheism can be justified by the inescapable demand for grounds. To believe there is a God, we have to have good grounds for the belief. But if no such grounds are provided, there exists no sufficient reason for believing in God, and the only reasonable position is to be a negative atheist or an agnostic (by negative atheist, I meant "a-theist," parallel to such words as *atypical* and *amoral*).

I must point out here what this "presumption" was not. It was not a scandalously prejudicial assumption of the conclusion needing to be proved. Rather, it was a procedural principle picking out the party upon whom the burden of proof should lie, much like the presumption of innocence that undergirds English Common Law.

I contended that in any properly systematic apologetic the propounder of a God hypothesis must begin, as would the propounder of any existential hypothesis, by first explaining the particular concept of God to be employed and then indicating how the corresponding object is to be identified. Only when and if these two essential preliminary tasks have been satisfactorily completed can it become sensible to begin deploying evidence intended to show that the concept does apply.

This argument garnered many and varied responses. Writing as an agnostic, the English philosopher Anthony Kenny maintained that there may be a presumption for agnosticism, but not for positive or negative atheism. He suggested that it takes more effort to show that you know something than that you do not (this includes even the claim that the concept of God is not coherent). But he said this does not let agnostics off the hook; a candidate for an examination may be able to justify the claim that he or she does not know the answer to one of the questions, but this does not enable the person to pass the examination.[8]

Kai Nielsen, a fellow atheist and former colleague of mine, cited a critic who alleged that the morally superior stance is to remain completely uncommitted until adequate reasons are produced. Nielsen then went on to say that I should show that believers and skeptics have a common concept of rationality with the criteria required to assess the merits of their differing claims. He added that there was "a large question mark before [my] presumption of atheism,"[9] if I did not produce a universally acceptable concept of rationality.

By far, the headiest challenge to the argument came from America. The modal logician Alvin Plantinga introduced the idea that theism is a properly basic belief. He asserted that belief in God is similar to belief in other basic truths, such as belief in other minds or perception (seeing a tree) or memory (belief in the past). In all these instances, you trust your cognitive faculties, although you cannot prove the truth of the belief in question. Similarly, people take certain propositions (e.g., the existence of the world) as basic and others as derivative from these basic propositions. Believers, it is argued, take the existence of God as a basic proposition.

The Thomist philosopher Ralph McInerny reasoned that it is natural for human beings to believe in God because of the order, arrangement, and lawlike character of natural events. So much so, he said, that the idea of God is almost innate, which seems like a prima facie argument against atheism. So, while Plantinga argued that theists did not bear the burden of proof, McInerny went still further, holding that the burden of proof must fall on atheists!

I should point out here that, unlike my other antitheological arguments, the argument for the presumption of atheism can be consistently accepted by theists. Given adequate grounds for belief in a God, theists commit no philosophical sin in so believing! The presumption of atheism is, at best, a methodological starting point, not an ontological conclusion.

CHANGING MY MIND

As a professional philosopher I have changed my mind on disputed topics more than once. This should not be surprising, of course, given my beliefs regarding the possibility of progress in philosophy and the principle of following the argument wherever it may lead me.

While teaching at the University of Keele in 1961, I wrote a book about Hume's *Inquiry Concerning Human Understanding* titled *Hume's Philosophy of Belief*. Up until then, Hume's *Inquiry* (usually called the first *Inquiry* to distinguish it from his later *Inquiry Concerning the Principles of Morals*) had usually been treated, in contrast to what the author himself thought of it, as a mere miscellany of after-thought essays. It is today considered Hume's greatest work. About my book on Hume, Gilbert Ryle said, "I think very highly of the book. It has scholarship and fire. Almost a record." And John Passmore said, "Any subsequent discussion of Hume's secularism will have to begin with Flew."

Despite these commendations, I have long wanted to make major corrections to my book *Hume's Philosophy of Belief*. One matter in particular calls for extensive corrections. The three chapters "The Idea of Necessary Connection," "Liberty and Necessity," and "Miracles and Methodology" all need to be rewritten in the light of my new-found awareness that Hume was utterly wrong to maintain that we have no experience, and hence no genuine ideas, of making things happen and of preventing things from happening, of physical necessity and of physical impossibility. Generations of Humeans have in consequence been misled into offering analyses of causation and of natural law that have been far too weak because they had no basis for accepting the existence of either cause and effect or natural laws. Meanwhile, in "Of Liberty and Necessity" and "Of Miracles," Hume himself was hankering after (even when he was not actually employing) notions of causes bringing about effects that were stronger than any that he was prepared to admit as legitimate.

Hume denied causation in the first *Inquiry* and claimed that all the external world really contains is constant conjunctions; that is, events of this sort are regularly followed by events of that sort. We notice these constant conjunctions and form strong habits associating the ideas of this with the ideas of that. We see water boiling when it is heated and associate the two. In thinking of real connections out there, however, we mistakenly project our own internal psychological associations. Hume's skepticism about cause and effect and his agnosticism about the external world are of course jettisoned the moment he leaves his study. Indeed, Hume jettisons all of his most radical skepticism even before he leaves his study. There is, for instance, no trace of the thesis that causal connections and necessities are nothing but false projections onto nature in the notorious section "Of Miracles" in the first *Inquiry*. Again in his *History of England* Hume gave no hint of skepticism about either the external world or causation. In this Hume may remind us of those of our own contemporaries who upon some sociological or philosophical grounds deny the possibility of objective knowledge. They then exempt from these corrosions of universal subjectivity their own political tirades, their own rather less abundant research work, and above all their own prime revelation that there can be no objective knowledge.

The other matter on which I changed my mind was free will, human freedom. This issue is important because the question of whether we are free lies at the heart of most major religions. In my earliest antitheological writings, I had drawn attention to the incongruity of evil in a universe created by an omnipotent, all-good Being. The theist response to this perceived incongruity was the claim that God gives humans free will, and that all or most of the obvious and scandalous evils are immediately or ultimately due to misuse of this dangerous gift, but that the end results will be the realization of a sum of greater goods than would otherwise be possible. I was, in fact, the first to label this the free-will defense.

But whether expressed as a debate between free will and predestination or, in secular suiting, free will and determinism, the question of whether we have free will is of fundamental importance. I responded by trying to have it both ways, by introducing a position now known as compatibilism. The incompatibilist says that thoroughgoing determinism is incompatible with free will. The compatibilist, on the other hand, maintains: not only can it be consistent to say both that someone will make a free choice and that the sense of that future choice is known beforehand to some future party, but also that free choices could be both free and choices even if they were physically caused to be made in the senses in which they are made, and even when their being made in these senses was determined by some law or laws of nature.

While still holding that people make free choices, in later years I came to see that you cannot at the same time consistently believe that these free choices are physically caused. In other words, compatibilism does not work. A law of nature is not a statement of a mere brute fact that one particular sort of happening will, as it happens, succeed or accompany some other sort of happening. It is, rather, a claim that an occurrence of one particular sort physically necessitates the occurrence of another sort such that it makes its nonoccurrence physically impossible. This is clearly not the case with a free choice.

We also need to distinguish two radically different senses of the word *cause,* with corresponding distinctions between senses of *determinism.* The causes of human actions are fundamentally, and most relevantly, different from the causes of all those events that are not human actions. Given the full cause of, say, an explosion, it becomes impossible for any power within the universe to prevent that explosion. But if I give you sufficient cause to celebrate, this does not necessitate your saying "Whoopee!" It follows from this that not every movement of human organisms can be completely determined by necessitating physical causes.

The two senses of *cause* can be distinguished using Hume's terminology of moral and physical causes. When we are talking of some altogether nonhuman event—an eclipse of the sun, say—then we employ the word *cause* in a sense implying both physical necessity and physical impossibility:

what happened was physically necessary and anything else was, in the circumstances, physically impossible.

Yet this is precisely not the case with the other sense of *cause,* the sense in which we speak of the causes (or reasons or motives) for human actions. Suppose, to use the example above, that I deliver some sort of good news to you. If you choose to respond to the news by celebrating, you may quite properly describe my action as the cause of your celebration. But I did not truly cause your celebration; it was not necessary and unavoidable. You may have chosen not to celebrate because we were, say, in a library at the time. To put it another way, my news may have resulted in your shouting "Whoopee!" But I did not unavoidably cause you to cry "Whoopee!" You might have said "Hooray!" instead. To adapt a famous phrase of the philosopher-mathematician Gottfried Leibniz, causes of this second, motivating sort *incline*, but do not *necessitate*.

Since Hume denied the legitimacy of the concept of physical necessity, he himself was unable to make this distinction in exactly the same way as it has been made here. Nevertheless, his choice of labels did point toward the fundamental difference between, on the one hand, the natural sciences and, on the other, the social and psychological.

Given these two fundamentally different senses of the word *cause,* it becomes clear that, at least while we are discussing the behavior of human beings, we now need to distinguish two correspondingly different senses of *deter-minism*: determination by *physical* causes and determination by *moral* causes. Certainly if a piece of behavior (what behaviorists call *behavior*) is fully determined by physical causes, then the behaver did not choose to behave in that way. Nor could he or she, at the time when that behavior occurred, have prevented it from occurring. But determination by moral causes is another matter. To explain individuals' conduct by reference to their reasons for—that is to say, moral causes of—their acting as they did is to presuppose that they could have acted differently. Desires and wants are certainly not irresistible conclusions as such. Most of us are sufficiently disciplined sometimes to refrain from doing things we very much want to do.

It is surely by failing these fundamental and crucial distinctions that so many people are misled into concluding that all explanations of conduct in terms of any kind of cause, physical or moral, supports an all-excusing doctrine of universal *physical* necessitation. This would mean that it was physically impossible for any to have behaved in any way other than the way they did.

What is required to avoid such errors is a logical analysis (such as one I carried out in *Social Life and Moral Judgment*) of the three intimately associated notions of being an agent, having a choice, and being able to do something other than what we actually do. In making a fundamental distinction between *movings* and *motions,* we become able to explain the equally fundamental concept of action. A moving is a movement that can be initiated or quashed at will; a motion is a movement that cannot. The power of moving is an attribute peculiar to people, whereas entities incapable of consciousness or intention can only manifest motion. Agents are creatures who, precisely and only insofar as they are agents, can and cannot but make choices: choices between the alternative courses of action or inaction that are from time to time open to them as individuals—real choices between genuine alternative possibilities. Agents, in their role as agents, inescapably must choose—can in no way avoid choosing—one of the two or usually many more options that on particular occasions are open and available to them.

The nerve of the distinction between the *movings* involved in an *action* and the *motions* that constitute necessitated behavior is that the latter behavior is physically necessitated, whereas the sense, the direction, and the character of *actions* as such are that, as a matter of logic, they necessarily cannot be physically necessitated (and as a matter of brute fact, they are not). It therefore becomes impossible to maintain the doctrine of universal physically necessitating determinism, the doctrine that says that all movements in the universe—including every human bodily movement, the *movings* as well as the *motions*—are determined by physically necessitating physical causes.

In the light of my defection from full compatibilism, much of the material I have published about free will or choice, both in religious and secular contexts, requires revision and correction. Given that the issue here concerns the second of what Kant called the three main questions of philosophy—God, freedom, and immortality—my change of my mind on this matter is fully as radical as my change on the question of God.

3

ATHEISM CALMLY CONSIDERED

He had been the league's premier player, first as a pitcher and then as a position player who hit twenty-nine home runs, while also pitching in seventeen games, in 1919. And then Boston Red Sox owner Harry Frazee, who some say needed cash to finance a Broadway play, sold George Herman "Babe" Ruth to the New York Yankees for $125,000 and other considerations. Ruth went on to lead the Yankees to seven American League pennants and four world championships. The Red Sox would not win their next World Series title until 2004, eighty-five years later.

Interestingly, 2004 was also the year I publicly revealed—in New York, as it happened—a "switch" of my own: after more than six decades of atheism, I announced that I had changed teams, so to speak. But in another sense, though I had come to see things from a different perspective, I was still playing the game with very much the same passion and principle as before.

A DUTY TO DIALOGUE

My case for atheism culminated with the publication of *The Presumption of Atheism*. In subsequent writings, I tackled entirely different themes and topics. In fact, in an essay for a 1986 book entitled *British Philosophy Today*, I commented that there were certainly other things I wanted to do, had I but world enough and time. For instance, I would have liked to explore the great historic disputes about the structure of the Trinity and about what is going on in the Eucharist. By the late 1960s, however, it had become clear to me that my services were urgently needed elsewhere. I knew that for the rest of my working life I must concentrate my energies in the broad secular areas of the philosophy of social science and social philosophy.

I issued one caveat, however. Since I had said much about the philosophy of religion over the years, I confessed that I remained intellectually duty bound to respond to challenge or criticism whenever possible, either admitting that I had gotten it wrong or explaining why I could not agree with my critics. This caveat, therefore, kept me engaged with defenders of theism who challenged my case for atheism, even as I moved on to other philosophical pursuits.

Such engagement was nothing new to me; in fact, my entire philosophical career has been spent in spirited dialogue and public debate with thinkers who differed from me on various questions ranging from social philosophy, the body-mind problem, and the free will–determinism dispute to the question of God. The themes under discussion in my debates on the existence of God evolved over the half century of my active intellectual life. In 1950 we sought to specify what it means to say "God loves you"; in 1976, we tried to clarify whether the concept of God was coherent; in 1985, we were trying to determine on whom fell the burden of proof; and in 1998 we were debating the implications of big-bang cosmology.

Through it all, however, my public engagements on theological themes not only helped to sharpen my own dialectic, but also introduced me to many colleagues and opponents worthy of my respect—and disagreement.

STICKING TO MY GUNS

Of all my debates, the two best attended were the debates of 1976 and 1998. The 1976 debate with Thomas Warren in Denton, Texas, had an audience, on different days, of five to seven thousand. The 1998 debate with William Lane Craig in Madison, Wisconsin, drew a crowd of about four thousand. These two events were the only times in my life in which I served as one of two protagonists in a formal public debate.

Debates in the United Kingdom typically took place before small academic audiences. Thus my first exposure to

a mass audience in the context of a debate was my encounter with the late Professor Thomas B. Warren, a Christian
philosopher. The debate was held on the campus of the
North Texas State University, now the University of North
Texas, in Denton, on four consecutive nights starting on
September 20, 1976, dates that coincided with the first of
that year's U.S. presidential debates between Jimmy Carter
and Gerald Ford. Before an enthusiastic audience, Dr.
Warren wielded an impressive array of charts and slides.

Interestingly, a good part of his case was an attack on
the theory of evolution, which at that time seemed to me
to be a novel undertaking. When Dr. Warren asked if I
believed there could be a being that is half ape and half
human, I responded that this was sort of like determining
whether someone is bald. My supervisor Gilbert Ryle was
positively egglike, and there is no doubt that everyone must
call that bald. But if we go one hair at a time, it is not easy
to define who is bald and who is not.

However, given my current views, a few of my very
declarative statements from that debate may be of interest
in depicting the fervency of my atheist convictions at that
point:

"I know there is no God."
"A system of belief about God" contains the same
"sort of contradiction" as "unmarried husbands or
round squares."

"I myself am inclined to believe that the universe
     was without beginning and will be without end.
     Indeed, I know of no good reasons for disputing
     either of these suggestions."
"I believe that living organisms evolved over an im-
     measurably long period from nonliving materials."

I was impressed with the hospitality of my hosts, but the
debate ended with both Warren and I sticking to our guns.

SHOOTOUT AT THE O.K. CORRAL

My next debate was nearly ten years later, and also in
Texas. It was held in Dallas in 1985 and felt like the famous
shootout at the O.K. Corral. I joined three other atheist
gunslingers: Wallace Matson, Kai Nielsen, and Paul Kurtz.
We battled a corresponding phalanx of leading theistic philosophers: Alvin Plantinga, William P. Alston, George Mavrodes, and Ralph McInerny.

Unlike the famous gun battle, however, this debate
provided no fireworks, because neither group was willing
to engage the other. Each side clung to the position that
the burden of proof was on the opposing side. I held to the
presumption of atheism derived from the old legal maxim
that "the onus of proof lies on the one who affirms, not on
the one who denies." Plantinga, on the theist side, insisted

that belief in God is properly basic, meaning that theists have no obligation to provide arguments for their belief, just as they cannot and do not have to produce arguments to support other fundamental beliefs like the existence of the world. As for my fellow atheists, Nielsen argued that philosophy of religion is boring and Matson that the traditional arguments for God were flawed; Kurtz contended that it is not possible to conclude from claims of divine revelation that there is a divine Revealer.

While in Dallas, I met two evangelical Christian philosophers, Terry Miethe, of the Oxford Study Center, and Gary Habermas, of Lynchburg College in Virginia, who have since become good friends. In subsequent years, I have had two published debates on the resurrection of Christ with Habermas and a debate on the existence of God with Miethe.

My side of the debate with Miethe was a restatement of many of the positions I had developed over the years on the coherence of the concept of God and the presumption of atheism. Miethe presented a formidable version of the cosmological argument that rested on the following premises:

Some limited, changing being(s) exist.

The present existence of every limited, changing being is caused by another.

There cannot be an infinite regress of causes of being, because an infinite regress of finite beings would not *cause* the existence of anything.

Therefore, there is a first Cause of the present existence of these beings.

The first Cause must be infinite, necessary, eternal,
and one.

The first uncaused Cause is identical with the God of
the Judeo-Christian tradition.

This argument rested not on the principle of sufficient reason, which I rejected, but on the principle of existential causality. I rejected this argument on the ground that the efficient causes in the universe are efficacious in their own right without the need for a first uncaused efficient Cause. I did say, however, that although "it is much more difficult to carry conviction with the contention that it is the mere continuing existence of the physical universe that requires some external explanation," nevertheless "it is easy to persuade the public that the original big bang required some kind of First (initiating) Cause."

HOLDING FAST

During the time I spent teaching at Bowling Green University in Ohio in the 1980s, I had a rather long debate with the philosopher Richard Swinburne, who, as noted earlier, had succeeded me at the University of Keele and then took over as the Nolloth Professor at Oxford.

Swinburne had emerged as the best-known defender of theism in the English-speaking world. A well-known skeptic and former colleague of mine, Terence Penelhum, had said of Swinburne's *The Coherence of Theism*: "I know of no defense against contemporary philosophical criticism that can compare with this one in quality of argumentation or clarity of thought."

One concept strongly defended by Swinburne was that of an omnipresent incorporeal spirit, one of the primary targets of my *God and Philosophy*. Like my debate with Plantinga, the debate with Swinburne also ended in a stalemate, with both of us holding fast to our starting points. I could make no sense of the concept of an incorporeal spirit, and Swinburne could not see why anyone would have a problem with it. My dialogue with Swinburne did not end there but, as will be apparent later in this book, continues to the present. (Incidentally, upon news of my change of mind on God, Plantinga remarked: "It speaks very well of Professor Flew's honesty. After all these years of opposing the idea of a Creator, he reverses his position on the basis of the evidence.")

The Swinburne debate was followed by the debate with William Lane Craig in 1998 in Madison, Wisconsin. The debate marked the fiftieth anniversary of the famous BBC debate on the existence of God between Bertrand Russell and Frederick Copleston. Craig argued that the origin of the universe and the complex order in the universe could best be explained by the existence of God. I responded that our knowledge of the universe must stop with the big bang, which is to be seen as the ultimate fact. As for the argument to design, I pointed out that even the most complex entities in the universe—human beings—are the products of unconscious physical and mechanical forces.

In this debate, I reiterated my position that an omnipotent God could make human beings in such a way that they would freely choose to obey him. This means that the traditional free-will defense cannot evade the consequence that God predestines all things, including free choices. I had always been repulsed by the doctrine of predestination, which holds that God predestines the damnation of most human beings. An important feature of this debate was Craig's rejection of traditional predestinarian ideas and his defense of libertarian free will. Craig held that God acts directly on effects and not on the secondary agents, and thus it was impossible for God to create a world of genuinely libertarian creatures who always do the right thing. He cited verses from the Bible that emphasize God's desire that "all persons should be saved" (e.g., 2 Peter 3:9). Quite recently I found out that John Wesley, whom I consider one of my country's great sons, had led a great controversy against predestination and in favor of the "Arminian" alternative, particularly in his greatest paper "Predestination

Calmly Considered." I also understand that many exegetes today see St. Paul's writings on predestination as referencing the role of specific individuals in the workings of the church and not their salvation or damnation.

MY NEW YORK DEBUT

The last of my public debates, a symposium at New York University, occurred in May 2004. The other participants were the Israeli scientist Gerald Schroeder, author of best sellers on science and religion, notably *The Science of God*, and the Scottish philosopher John Haldane, whose *Theism and Atheism* was a debate on God's existence with my friend Jack Smart.

To the surprise of all concerned, I announced at the start that I now accepted the existence of a God. What might have been an intense exchange of opposing views ended up as a joint exploration of the developments in modern science that seemed to point to a higher Intelligence. In the video of the symposium, the announcer suggested that of all the great discoveries of modern science, the greatest was God.

In this symposium, when asked if recent work on the origin of life pointed to the activity of a creative Intelligence, I said:

Yes, I now think it does ... almost entirely because of the DNA investigations. What I think the DNA material has done is that it has shown, by the almost unbelievable complexity of the arrangements which are needed to produce (life), that intelligence must have been involved in getting these extraordinarily diverse elements to work together. It's the enormous complexity of the number of elements and the enormous subtlety of the ways they work together. The meeting of these two parts at the right time by chance is simply minute. It is all a matter of the enormous complexity by which the results were achieved, which looked to me like the work of intelligence.

This statement represented a major change of course for me, but it was nevertheless consistent with the principle I have embraced since the beginning of my philosophical life—of following the argument no matter where it leads.

I was particularly impressed with Gerry Schroeder's point-by-point refutation of what I call the "monkey theorem." This idea, which has been presented in a number of forms and variations, defends the possibility of life arising by chance using the analogy of a multitude of monkeys banging away on computer keyboards and eventually ending up writing a Shakespearean sonnet.

Schroeder first referred to an experiment conducted by the British National Council of Arts. A computer was placed in a cage with six monkeys. After one month of hammering away at it (as well as using it as a bathroom!), the monkeys produced fifty typed pages—but not a single word. Schroeder noted that this was the case even though the shortest word in the English language is one letter (*a* or *I*). *A* is a word only if there is a space on either side of it. If we take it that the keyboard has thirty characters (the twenty-six letters and other symbols), then the likelihood of getting a one-letter word is 30 times 30 times 30, which is 27,000. The likelihood of a getting a one-letter word is one chance out of 27,000.

Schroeder then applied the probabilities to the sonnet analogy. "What's the chance of getting a Shakespearean sonnet?" he asked. He continued:

All the sonnets are the same length. They're by definition fourteen lines long. I picked the one I knew the opening line for, "Shall I compare thee to a summer's day?" I counted the number of letters; there are 488 letters in that sonnet. What's the likelihood of hammering away and getting 488 letters in the exact sequence as in "Shall I Compare Thee to a Summer's Day?"? What you end up with is 26 multiplied by itself 488 times—or 26 to the 488th power. Or, in other words, in base 10, 10 to the 690th.

[Now] the number of particles in the universe—not grains of sand, I'm talking about protons, electrons, and neutrons—is 10 to the 80th. Ten to the 80th is 1 with 80 zeros after it. Ten to the 690th is 1 with 690 zeros after it. There are not enough particles in the universe to write down the trials; you'd be off by a factor of 10 to the 600th.

If you took the entire universe and converted it to computer chips—forget the monkeys—each one weighing a millionth of a gram and had each computer chip able to spin out 488 trials at, say, a million times a second; if you turn the entire universe into these microcomputer chips and these chips were spinning a million times a second [producing] random letters, the number of trials you would get since the beginning of time would be 10 to the 90th trials. It would be off again by a factor of 10 to the 600th. You will never get a sonnet by chance. The universe would have to be 10 to the 600th times larger. Yet the world just thinks the monkeys can do it every time.[1]

After hearing Schroeder's presentation, I told him that he had very satisfactorily and decisively established that the "monkey theorem" was a load of rubbish, and that it was particularly good to do it with just a sonnet; the theorem is sometimes proposed using the works of Shakespeare or a single play, such as *Hamlet*. If the theorem won't work for a single sonnet, then of course it's simply absurd to suggest that the more elaborate feat of the origin of life could have been achieved by chance.

DUELING WITH DAWKINS

In addition to my public debates, I have engaged in various polemical discussions in writing. One prominent instance of such discussions is the exchanges I have had with the scientist Richard Dawkins. Although I commended his atheist works, I have always been a critic of his selfish-gene school of thought.

In my book *Darwinian Evolution,* I pointed out that natural selection does not positively produce anything. It only eliminates, or tends to eliminate, whatever is not competitive. A variation does not need to bestow any actual competitive advantage in order to avoid elimination; it is sufficient that it does not burden its owner with any competitive *dis*advantage. To choose a rather silly illustration, suppose I have useless wings tucked away under my suit coat, wings that are too weak to lift my frame off the ground. Useless as they are, these wings do not enable me to escape predators or gather food. But as long as they don't make me *more* vulnerable to predators, I will probably survive to reproduce and pass on my wings to my descendants. Darwin's mistake in drawing too positive an inference with his suggestion that natural selection produces something was perhaps due to his employment of the expressions "natural selection" or "survival of the fittest" rather than his own ultimately preferred alternative, "natural preservation."

I went on to remark that Richard Dawkins's *The Selfish Gene* was a major exercise in popular mystification. As an atheist philosopher, I considered this work of popularization as destructive in its own ways as either *The Naked Ape* or *The Human Zoo* by Desmond Morris. In his works, Morris offers as the results of zoological illumination what amounts to a systematic denial of all that is most peculiar to our species contemplated as a biological phenomenon. He ignores or explains away the obvious differences between human beings and other species.

Dawkins, on the other hand, labored to discount or depreciate the upshot of fifty or more years' work in genetics—the discovery that the observable traits of organisms are for the most part conditioned by the interactions of many genes, while most genes have manifold effects on many such traits. For Dawkins, the main means for producing human behavior is to attribute to genes characteristics that can significantly be attributed only to persons. Then, after insisting that we are all the choiceless creatures of our genes, he infers that we cannot help but share the unlovely personal characteristics of those all-controlling monads.

Genes, of course, can be neither selfish nor unselfish any more than they or any other nonconscious entities can engage in competition or make selections. (Natural selection is, notoriously, not selection; and it is a somewhat less familiar logical fact that, below the human level, the struggle for existence is not "competitive" in the true sense of the word.) But this did not stop Dawkins from proclaiming that his book "is not science fiction; it is science.... We are survival machines—robot vehicles blindly programmed to preserve the selfish molecules known as genes."[2] Although he later issued occasional disavowals, Dawkins gave no warning in his book against taking him literally. He added, sensationally, that "the argument of this book is that we, and all other animals, are machines created by our genes."

If any of this were true, it would be no use to go on, as Dawkins does, to preach: "Let us try to teach generosity and altruism, because we are born selfish." No eloquence can move programmed robots. But in fact none of it is true—or even faintly sensible. Genes, as we have seen, do not and cannot necessitate our conduct. Nor are they capable of the calculation and understanding required to plot a course of either ruthless selfishness or sacrificial compassion.

PLAYING WITH PASSION AND PRINCIPLE

Babe Ruth retired from baseball at the age of forty. I am more than twice that age now, and although I have changed my position on the existence of God, I hope my defense of atheism and debates with theists and others indicate my enduring interest in the questions of theology and my willingness to continue exploring various answers. Analysts and psychologists can make of this what they will, but the impetus for me is still what it has always been: the pursuit of valid arguments with true conclusions.

I hope I can play with as much passion and principle as I always have in the next part of the book, as I lay out my present position and the body of evidence that led me to affirm it.

PART II

MY DISCOVERY
OF THE DIVINE

4

A PILGRIMAGE OF REASON

L et us begin with a parable. Imagine that a satellite phone is washed ashore on a remote island inhabited by a tribe that has never had contact with modern civilization. The natives play with the numbers on the dial pad and hear different voices upon hitting certain sequences. They assume first that it's the device that makes these noises. Some of the cleverer natives, the scientists of the tribe, assemble an exact replica and hit the numbers again. They hear the voices again. The conclusion seems obvious to them. This particular combination of crystals and metals and chemicals produces what seems like human voices, and this means that the voices are simply properties of the device.

But the tribal sage summons the scientists for a discussion. He has thought long and hard on the matter and has reached the following conclusion: the voices coming through the instrument must be coming from people like themselves, people who are living and conscious although speaking in another language. Instead of assuming that the voices are simply properties of the handset, they should investigate the possibility that through some mysterious communication network they are "in touch" with other humans. Perhaps further study along these lines could lead to a greater understanding of the world beyond their island. But the scientists simply laugh at the sage and say: "Look, when we damage the instrument, the voices stop coming. So they're obviously nothing more than sounds produced by a unique combination of lithium and printed circuit boards and light-emitting diodes."

In this parable we see how easy it is to let preconceived theories shape the way we view evidence instead of letting the evidence shape our theories. A Copernician leap may thus be prevented by a thousand Ptolemaic epicycles. (Defenders of Ptolemy's geocentric model of the solar system resisted Copernicus' heliocentric model by using the concept of epicycles to explain away observations of planetary motion that conflicted with their model.) And in this, it seems to me, lies the peculiar danger, the endemic evil, of dogmatic atheism. Take such utterances as "We should not ask for an explanation of how it is that the world exists; it is here and that's all" or "Since we cannot accept a transcendent source of life, we choose to believe the impossible: that life arose spontaneously by chance from matter" or "The laws of physics are 'lawless laws' that arise from the void—end of discussion." They look at first sight like rational arguments that have a special authority because they have a no-nonsense air about them. Of course, this is no more sign that they are either rational or arguments.

Now to make a rational argument that such and such is the case is necessarily to provide reasons to support one's case. Suppose then that we are in doubt what someone who gives vent to an utterance of this sort is arguing, or suppose that, more radically, we are skeptical about whether they are really arguing anything at all, one way of trying to understand their utterance is to attempt to find what evidence, if any, they offer to support the truth of their claims. For if the utterance is indeed rational and an argument, it must indeed provide reasons in its favor from science or philosophy. And anything that would count against the utterance, or which would induce the speaker to withdraw it and to admit that it had been mistaken, must be laid out. But if there is no reason and no evidence offered in its support, then there is no reason or evidence that it is a rational argument.

When the Sage in the parable tells the scientists to investigate all dimensions of the evidence, he was suggesting that a failure to explore what seems prima facie reasonable and promising ipso facto precludes the possibility of a greater understanding of the world beyond the island inhabited by the tribe.

Now it often seems to people who are not atheists as if there is no conceivable piece of evidence that would be admitted by apparently scientific-minded dogmatic atheists to be a sufficient reason for conceding "There might be a God after all." I therefore put to my former fellow-atheists the simple central question: "What would have to occur or to have occurred to constitute for you a reason to at least consider the existence of a superior Mind?"

LAYING THE CARDS ON THE TABLE

Moving on now from the parable, it's time for me to lay my cards on the table, to set out my own views and the reasons that support them. I now believe that the universe was brought into existence by an infinite Intelligence. I believe that this universe's intricate laws manifest what scientists have called the Mind of God. I believe that life and reproduction originate in a divine Source.

Why do I believe this, given that I expounded and defended atheism for more than a half century? The short answer is this: this is the world picture, as I see it, that has emerged from modern science. Science spotlights three dimensions of nature that point to God. The first is the fact that nature obeys laws. The second is the dimension of life, of intelligently organized and purpose-driven beings, which arose from matter. The third is the very existence of nature. But it is not science alone that has guided me. I have also been helped by a renewed study of the classical philosophical arguments.

My departure from atheism was not occasioned by any new phenomenon or argument. Over the last two decades, my whole framework of thought has been in a state of migration. This was a consequence of my continuing assessment of the evidence of nature. When I finally came to recognize the existence of a God, it was not a paradigm shift, because my paradigm remains, as Plato in his *Republic* scripted his Socrates to insist: "We must follow the argument wherever it leads."

You might ask how I, a philosopher, could speak to issues treated by scientists. The best way to answer this is with another question. Are we engaging in science or philosophy here? When you study the interaction of two physical bodies, for instance, two subatomic particles, you are engaged in science. When you ask how it is that those subatomic particles—or *anything* physical—could exist and why, you are engaged in philosophy. When you draw philosophical conclusions from scientific data, then you are thinking as a philosopher.

THINKING AS A PHILOSOPHER

So let's apply the above insight here. In 2004 I said that the origin of life cannot be explained if you start with matter alone. My critics responded by triumphantly announcing that I had not read a particular paper in a scientific journal or followed a brand-new development relating to abiogenesis (the spontaneous generation of life from nonliving material). In doing so, they missed the whole point. My concern was not with this or that fact of chemistry or genetics, but with the fundamental question of what it means for something to be alive and how this relates to the body of chemical and genetic facts viewed as a whole. To think at this level is to think as a philosopher. And, at the risk of sounding immodest, I must say that this is properly the job of philosophers, not of the scientists as scientists; the competence specific to scientists gives no advantage when it comes to considering this question, just as a star baseball player has no special competence on the dental benefits of a particular toothpaste.

Of course, scientists are just as free to think as philosophers as anyone else. And, of course, not all scientists will agree with my particular interpretation of the facts they generate. But their disagreements will have to stand on their own two philosophical feet. In other words, if they are engaged in philosophical analysis, neither their

authority nor their expertise as scientists is of any relevance. This should be easy to see. If they present their
views on the economics of science, such as making claims
about the number of jobs created by science and tech-
nology, they will have to make their case in the court of
economic analysis. Likewise, a scientist who speaks as a
philosopher will have to furnish a philosophical case. As
Albert Einstein himself said, "The man of science is a
poor philosopher."[1]

Happily, this is not always the case. The leaders of science over the last hundred years, along with some of today's
most influential scientists, have built a philosophically
compelling vision of a rational universe that sprang from
a divine Mind. As it happens, this is the particular view of
the world that I now find to be the soundest philosophical
explanation of a multitude of phenomena encountered by
scientists and laypeople alike.

Three domains of scientific inquiry have been especially
important for me, and I will consider them as we proceed in
the light of today's evidence. The first is the question that
puzzled and continues to puzzle most reflective scientists:
How did the laws of nature come to be? The second is evident to all: How did life as a phenomenon originate from
nonlife? And the third is the problem that philosophers
handed over to cosmologists: How did the universe, by
which we mean all that is physical, come into existence?

A RECOVERY OF WISDOM

As for my new position on the classical philosophical debates about God, in this area I was persuaded above all by the philosopher David Conway's argument for God's existence in his book *The Recovery of Wisdom: From Here to Antiquity in Quest of Sophia*. Conway is a distinguished British philosopher at Middlesex University who is equally at home with classical and modern philosophy.

The God whose existence is defended by Conway and myself is the God of Aristotle. Conway writes:

> In sum, to the Being whom he considered to be the explanation of the world and its broad form, Aristotle ascribed the following attributes: immutability, immateriality, omnipotence, omniscience, oneness or indivisibility, perfect goodness and necessary existence. There is an impressive correspondence between this set of attributes and those traditionally ascribed to God within the Judaeo-Christian tradition. It is one that fully justifies us in viewing Aristotle as having had the same Divine Being in mind as the cause of the world that is the object of worship of these two religions.[2]

As Conway sees it, then, the God of the monotheistic religions has the same attributes as the God of Aristotle.

In his book, Conway attempts to defend what he describes as the "classical conception of philosophy." That conception is "the view that the explanation of the world and its broad form is that it is the creation of a supreme omnipotent and omniscient intelligence, more commonly referred to as God, who created it in order to bring into existence and sustain rational beings."[3] God created the world so as to bring into being a race of rational creatures. Conway believes, and I concur, that it is possible to learn of the existence and nature of this Aristotelian God by the exercise of unaided human reason.

I must stress that my discovery of the Divine has proceeded on a purely natural level, without any reference to supernatural phenomena. It has been an exercise in what is traditionally called natural theology. It has had no connection with any of the revealed religions. Nor do I claim to have had any personal experience of God or any experience that may be called supernatural or miraculous. In short, my discovery of the Divine has been a pilgrimage of reason and not of faith.

5

WHO WROTE THE LAWS OF NATURE?

Perhaps the most popular and intuitively plausible argument for God's existence is the so-called argument from design. According to this argument, the design that is apparent in nature suggests the existence of a cosmic Designer. I have often stressed that this is actually an argument *to* design *from* order, as such arguments proceed from the perceived order in nature to show evidence of design and, thus, a Designer. Although I was once sharply critical of the argument to design, I have since come to see that, when correctly formulated, this argument constitutes a persuasive case for the existence of God. Developments in two areas in particular have led me to this conclusion. The first is the question of the origin of the laws of nature and the related insights of eminent modern scientists. The second is the question of the origin of life and reproduction.

What do I mean by the laws of nature? By *law*, I simply mean a regularity or symmetry in nature. Some common textbook examples should show what I mean:

> Boyle's law stipulates that, given constant temperature, the product of the volume and pressure of a fixed quantity of an ideal gas is constant.
>
> According to Newton's first law of motion, an object at rest will remain at rest unless acted upon by an external and unbalanced force; an object in motion will remain in motion unless acted upon by an external and unbalanced force.
>
> According to the law of the conservation of energy, the total amount of energy in an isolated system remains constant.

The important point is not merely that there are regularities in nature, but that these regularities are mathematically precise, universal, and "tied together." Einstein spoke of them as "reason incarnate." The question we should ask is how nature came packaged in this fashion. This is certainly the question that scientists from Newton to Einstein to Heisenberg have asked—and answered. Their answer was the Mind of God.

Now, this way of thinking is not something found only in well-known premodern theistic scientists like Isaac

Newton and James Maxwell. On the contrary, many prominent scientists of the modern era have regarded the laws
of nature as thoughts of the Mind of God. Stephen
Hawking ends his best-selling *A Brief History of Time*
with this passage:

> If we discover a complete theory, it should in time
> be understandable by everyone, not just by a few
> scientists. Then we shall all, philosophers, scien-
> tists and just ordinary people, be able to take part
> in the discussion of the question of why it is that
> we and the universe exist. If we find the answer
> to that, it would be the ultimate triumph of hu-
> man reason—for then we should know the mind
> of God.

On the previous page he asked: "Even if there is only one
possible unified theory, it is just a set of rules and equations. What is it that breathes fire into the equations and
makes a universe for them to describe?"[1]

Hawking had more to say on this in later interviews:
"The overwhelming impression is one of order. The more
we discover about the universe, the more we find that it is
governed by rational laws." And, "You still have the question: why does the universe bother to exist? If you like, you
can define God to be the answer to that question."[2]

WHO WROTE ALL THOSE BOOKS?

Long before Hawking, Einstein had used similar language: "I want to know how God created this world.... I want to know His thoughts, the rest are details."[3] In my book *God and Philosophy*, I had said we cannot make too much of these sorts of passages, since Einstein had said that he believed in Spinoza's God.[4] Since for Baruch Spinoza the words *God* and *nature* were synonymous, it could be said that Einstein, in the eyes of Judaism, Christianity, and Islam, was unequivocally an atheist and that he was "a spiritual father of all atheists."

But the recent book *Einstein and Religion*, by one of Einstein's friends, Max Jammer, paints a very different picture of the influence of Spinoza and also of Einstein's own beliefs. Jammer shows that Einstein's knowledge of Spinoza was quite limited; he had read only Spinoza's *Ethics* and turned down repeated requests to write about Spinoza's philosophy. In response to one request, he replied, "I do not have the professional knowledge to write a scholarly article about Spinoza."[5] Although Einstein shared Spinoza's belief in determinism, Jammer holds that it "is artificial and unwarranted" to assume that Spinoza's thought influenced Einstein's science.[6] Jammer notes too that "Einstein felt akin to Spinoza because he realized that they shared a need for solitude as well as the fate of having been reared within

the Jewish heritage but having become subsequently alien-
ated from its religious heritage."[7]

While drawing attention to Spinoza's pantheism, Einstein, in fact, expressly denied being either an atheist or a
pantheist:

> *I'm not an atheist, and I don't think I can call my-*
> *self a pantheist.* We are in the position of a little
> child entering a huge library filled with books in
> many languages. The child knows someone must
> have written those books. It does not know how. It
> does not understand the languages in which they
> are written. The child dimly suspects a mysterious
> order in the arrangement of the books but doesn't
> know what it is. That, it seems to me, is the attitude
> of even the most intelligent human being toward
> God. We see the universe marvelously arranged
> and obeying certain laws but only dimly understand
> these laws. Our limited minds grasp the mysteri-
> ous force that moves the constellations. [Emphasis
> added.][8]

In his book *The God Delusion,* Richard Dawkins pro-
pounds my old position that Einstein was an atheist. In
doing so, Dawkins ignores Einstein's categorical statement
above that he was neither an atheist nor a pantheist. This

is puzzling because Dawkins cites Jammer on occasion, but leaves out numerous statements by Jammer and Einstein that are fatal to his own case. Jammer observes, for instance, that "Einstein always protested against being regarded as an atheist. In a conversation with Prince Hubertus of Lowenstein, for example, he declared, 'What really makes me angry is that they [people who say there is no God] quote me for support of their views.' Einstein renounced atheism because he never considered his denial of a personal God as a denial of God."[9]

Einstein, of course, did not believe in a personal God. But he said:

> It is a different question whether belief in a personal God should be contested. Freud endorsed this view in his latest publication. I myself would never engage in such a task. For such a belief seems to me preferable to any lack of any transcendental outlook of life, and I wonder whether one can ever successfully render to the majority of mankind a more sublime means in order to satisfy its metaphysical needs.[10]

"To sum up," concludes Jammer, "Einstein, like Maimonides and Spinoza, categorically rejected any anthropomorphism in religious thought." But unlike Spinoza, who saw the only logical consequence of the denial of a personal God in an identification of God with nature, Einstein maintained that God manifests himself "in the laws of the universe as a spirit vastly superior to that of man, and one in the face of which we with our modest powers must feel humble." Einstein agreed with Spinoza that he who knows nature knows God, but not because nature is God, but because the pursuit of science in studying nature leads to religion.[11]

EINSTEIN'S "SUPERIOR MIND"

Einstein clearly believed in a transcendent source of the rationality of the world that he variously called "superior mind," "illimitable superior spirit," "superior reasoning force," and "mysterious force that moves the constellations." This is evident in several of his statements:

I have never found a better expression than "religious" for this trust in the rational nature of reality and of its peculiar accessibility to the human mind. Where this trust is lacking science degenerates into an uninspired procedure. Let the devil care if the priests make capital out of this. There is no remedy for that.[12]

Whoever has undergone the intense experience of successful advances in this domain [science] is moved by profound reverence for the rationality made manifest in existence ... the grandeur of reason incarnate in existence.[13]

Certain it is that a conviction, akin to religious feeling, of the rationality or intelligibility of the world lies behind all scientific work of a higher order.... This firm belief, a belief bound up with deep feeling, in a superior mind that reveals itself in the world of experience, represents my conception of God.[14]

Every one who is seriously engaged in the pursuit of science becomes convinced that the laws of nature manifest the existence of a spirit vastly superior to that of men, and one in the face of which we with our modest powers must feel humble.[15]

My religiosity consists of a humble admiration of the infinitely superior spirit who reveals himself in the slight details we are able to perceive with our frail and feeble minds. That deeply emotional conviction of the presence of a superior reasoning power, which is revealed in the incomprehensible universe, forms my idea of God.[16]

QUANTUM LEAPS TOWARD GOD

Einstein, the discoverer of relativity, was not the only great scientist who saw a connection between the laws of nature and the Mind of God. The progenitors of quantum physics, the other great scientific discovery of modern times, Max Planck, Werner Heisenberg, Erwin Schrödinger, and Paul Dirac, have all made similar statements,[17] and I reproduce a few of these below.

Werner Heisenberg, famous for Heisenberg's uncertainty principle and matrix mechanics, said, "In the course of my life I have repeatedly been compelled to ponder on the relationship of these two regions of thought [science and religion], for I have never been able to doubt the reality of that to which they point."[18] On another occasion he said:

Wolfgang [Pauli] asked me quite unexpectedly: "Do you believe in a personal God?"... "May I rephrase your question?" I asked. "I myself should prefer the following formulation: Can you, or anyone else, reach the central order of things or events, whose existence seems beyond doubt, as directly as you can reach the soul of another human being. I am using the term 'soul' quite deliberately so as not to be misunderstood. If you put your question like that, I would say yes.... If the magnetic force that has guided this particular compass—and what else was its source but the central order?—should ever become extinguished, terrible things may happen to mankind, far more terrible even than concentration camps and atom bombs."[19]

Another quantum pioneer, Erwin Schrödinger, who developed wave mechanics, stated:

The scientific picture of the world around me is very deficient. It gives me a lot of factual information, puts all our experience in a magnificently consistent order, but is ghastly silent about all that is really near to our heart, that really matters to us. It cannot tell a word about the sensation of red and blue, bitter and sweet, feelings of delight and sorrow. It knows nothing of beauty and ugly, good or bad, God and eternity. Science sometimes pretends to answer questions in these domains, but the answers are very often so silly that we are not inclined to take them seriously.

Science is reticent too when it is a question of the great Unity of which we somehow form a part, to which we belong. The most popular name for it in our time is God, with a capital "G." Science is, very usually, branded as being atheistic. After what we have said this is not astonishing. If its world picture does not even contain beauty, delight, sorrow, if personality is cut out of it by agreement, how should it contain the most sublime idea that presents itself to the human mind.[20]

Max Planck, who first introduced the quantum hypothesis, unambiguously held that science complements religion, contending, "There can never be any real opposition between religion and science; for the one is the complement of the other."[21] He also said, "Religion and natural science are fighting a joint battle in an incessant, never relaxing crusade against skepticism and against dogmatism, against unbelief and superstition ... [and therefore] 'On to God!'"[22]

Paul A. M. Dirac, who complemented Heisenberg and Schrödinger with a third formulation of quantum theory, observed that "God is a mathematician of a very high order and He used advanced mathematics in constructing the universe."[23]

Generations before any of these scientists, Charles Darwin had already expressed a similar view:

> [Reason tells me of the] extreme difficulty or rather impossibility of conceiving this immense and wonderful universe, including man with his capability of looking far backwards and far into futurity, as the result of blind chance or necessity. When thus reflecting I feel compelled to look to a First Cause having an intelligent mind in some degree analogous to that of man; and I deserve to be called a Theist.[24]

This train of thought has been kept alive in the present time in the writings of many of today's leading expositors of science. These range from scientists like Paul Davies, John Barrow, John Polkinghorne, Freeman Dyson, Francis Collins, Owen Gingerich, and Roger Penrose to philosophers of science like Richard Swinburne and John Leslie.

Davies and Barrow, in particular, have further developed the insights of Einstein, Heisenberg, and other scientists into theories about the relationship between the rationality of nature and the Mind of God. Both have received the Templeton Prize for their contributions to this exploration.

Their works correct many common misconceptions while shedding light on the issues discussed here.

WHOSE LAWS?

In his Templeton address, Paul Davies makes the point that "science can proceed only if the scientist adopts an essentially theological worldview." Nobody asks where the laws of physics come from, but "even the most atheistic scientist accepts as an act of faith the existence of a lawlike order in nature that is at least in part comprehensible to us." Davies rejects two common misconceptions. He says the idea that a theory of everything would show that this is the only logically consistent world is "demonstrably wrong," because there is no evidence at all that the universe is logically necessary, and in fact it is possible to imagine alternative universes that are logically consistent. Second, he says it is "arrant nonsense" to suppose that the laws of physics are our laws and not nature's. Physicists will not believe that Newton's inverse law of gravitation is a cultural creation. He holds that the laws of physics "really exist," and scientists' job is to uncover and not invent them.

Davies draws attention to the fact that the laws of nature underlying phenomena are not found through direct observation, but extracted through experiment and mathematical theory. The laws are written in a cosmic code that scientists must crack in order to reveal the message that is "nature's message, God's message, take your choice, but not *our* message."

The burning question, he says, is threefold:

Where do the laws of physics come from?
Why is it that we have these laws instead of some other set?
How is that we have a set of laws that drives feature-less gases to life, consciousness and intelligence?

These laws "seem almost contrived—fine-tuned, some commentators have claimed—so that life and conscious-ness may emerge." He concludes that this "contrived nature of physical existence is just too fantastic for me to take on board as simply 'given.' It points to a deeper under-lying meaning to existence." Such words as *purpose* and *design,* he says, only capture imperfectly what the universe is about. "But, that it is about something, I have absolutely no doubt."[25]

John Barrow, in his Templeton address, observes that the unending complexity and exquisite structure of the universe are governed by a few simple laws that are sym-metrical and intelligible. In fact, "there are mathematical equations, little squiggles on pieces of paper, that tell us how whole universes behave." Like Davies, he dismisses the idea that the order of the universe is imposed by our minds. Moreover, "natural selection requires no understanding of quarks and black holes for our survival and multiplication."

Barrow observes that in the history of science new theories extend and subsume old ones. Although Newton's theory of mechanics and gravity has been superseded by Einstein's and will be succeeded by some other theory in the future, a thousand years from now engineers will still rely on Newton's theories. Likewise, he says, religious conceptions of the universe also use approximations and analogies to help in grasping ultimate things. "They are not the whole truth, but this does not stop them being a part of the truth."[26]

THE DIVINE LAWMAKER

A few philosophers have also written about the divine provenance of the laws of nature. In his book *The Divine Lawmaker: Lectures on Induction, Laws of Nature and the Existence of God*, Oxford philosopher John Foster contends that regularities in nature, however you describe them, can be best explained by a divine Mind. If you accept the fact that there are laws, then something must impose that regularity on the universe. What agent (or agents) brings this about? He contends that the theistic option is the only serious option as the source, so that "we shall be rationally warranted in concluding that it is God—the God of the theistic account—who creates the laws by imposing the regularities on the world as regularities." Even if you deny the existence of laws, he argues, "there is a strong case for explaining the regularities by appealing to the agency of God."[27]

Swinburne makes a related point in a response to Dawkins's critique of his argument to design:

What is a law of nature? (This is not an issue faced by any of my critics.) To say that it is a law of nature that all bodies behave in a certain way (e.g., attract each other in accord with a certain formula) is, I suggest, just to say that each body of physical necessity behaves in that way (e.g., attracts each body in that way). And it is simpler to suppose that this uniformity arises from the action of one substance which causes them all to behave in the same way, rather than to suppose that all bodies behaving in the same uniform way is an ultimate brute fact.[28]

Swinburne's central argument is that a personal God with the traditional properties best explains the operation of the laws of nature.

Richard Dawkins has rejected this argument on the grounds that God is too complex a solution for explaining the universe and its laws. This strikes me as a bizarre thing to say about the concept of an omnipotent spiritual Being. What is complex about the idea of an omnipotent and omniscient Spirit, an idea so simple that it is understood by all the adherents of the three great monotheistic religions— Judaism, Christianity, and Islam? Commenting on Dawkins, Alvin Plantinga recently pointed out that, by Dawkins's own definition, God is simple—not complex—because God is a spirit, not a material object, and hence does not have parts.

Returning to my parable of the satellite phone in the previous chapter, the laws of nature pose a problem for atheists because they are a voice of rationality heard through the mechanisms of matter. "Science is based on the assumption that the universe is thoroughly rational and logical at all levels," writes Paul Davies, arguably the most influential contemporary expositor of modern science. "Atheists claim that the laws [of nature] exist reasonlessly and that the universe is ultimately absurd. As a scientist, I find this hard to accept. There must be an unchanging rational ground in which the logical, orderly nature of the universe is rooted."[29]

Those scientists who point to the Mind of God do not merely advance a series of arguments or a process of syllogistic reasoning. Rather, they propound a vision of reality that emerges from the conceptual heart of modern science and imposes itself on the rational mind. It is a vision that I personally find compelling and irrefutable.

6

DID THE UNIVERSE KNOW WE WERE COMING?

Imagine entering a hotel room on your next vacation. The CD player on the bedside table is softly playing a track from your favorite recording. The framed print over the bed is identical to the image that hangs over the fireplace at home. The room is scented with your favorite fragrance. You shake your head in amazement and drop your bags on the floor.

You're suddenly very alert. You step over to the minibar, open the door, and stare in wonder at the contents. Your favorite beverages. Your favorite cookies and candy. Even the brand of bottled water you prefer.

You turn from the minibar, then, and gaze around the room. You notice the book on the desk: it's the latest volume by your favorite author. You glance into the bathroom, where personal care and grooming products are lined up on the counter, each one as if it was chosen specifically for you. You switch on the television; it is tuned to your favorite channel.

Chances are, with each new discovery about your hospitable new environment, you would be less inclined to think it was all a mere coincidence, right? You might wonder how the hotel managers acquired such detailed information about you. You might marvel at their meticulous preparation. You might even double-check what all this is going to cost you. But you would certainly be inclined to believe that someone knew you were coming.

OUR FINELY TUNED UNIVERSE

That vacation scenario is a clumsy, limited parallel to the so-called fine-tuning argument. The recent popularity of this argument has highlighted a new dimension of the laws of nature. "The more I examine the universe and study the details of its architecture," writes physicist Freeman Dyson, "the more evidence I find that the universe in some sense knew we were coming."[1] In other words, the laws of nature seem to have been crafted so as to move the universe toward the emergence and sustenance of life. This is the anthropic principle, popularized by such thinkers as Martin Rees, John Barrow, and John Leslie.

Let's take the most basic laws of physics. It has been calculated that if the value of even one of the fundamental constants—the speed of light or the mass of an electron, for instance—had been to the slightest degree different, then no planet capable of permitting the evolution of human life could have formed.

This fine tuning has been explained in two ways. Some scientists have said the fine tuning is evidence for divine design; many others have speculated that our universe is one of multiple others—a "multiverse"—with the difference that ours happened to have the right conditions for life. Virtually no major scientist today claims that the fine tuning was purely a result of chance factors at work in a single universe.

In his book *Infinite Minds*, John Leslie, a leading anthropic theorist, argues that fine tuning is best explained by divine design. He says that he is impressed not by particular arguments for instances of fine tuning, but by the fact that these arguments exist in such profusion. "If, then, there were aspects of nature's workings that appeared very fortunate and also entirely fundamental," he writes, "then these might well be seen as evidence specially favoring belief in God."[2] He cites examples of such "fortunate" and "fundamental" aspects of nature's workings:

1   The principle of special relativity ensures that forc-
     es such as electromagnetism have an invariable
     effect regardless of whether they act at right angles
     to a system's direction of travel. This enables
     genetic codes to work and planets to hold together
     when rotating.

2   Quantum laws prevent electrons from spiraling
     into atomic nuclei.

3   Electromagnetism has one-force strength, which
     enables multiple key processes to take place: it
     allows stars to burn steadily for billions of years; it
     enables carbon synthesis in stars; it ensures that
     leptons do not replace quarks, which would have
     made atoms impossible; it is responsible for protons
     not decaying too fast or repelling each other too
     strongly, which would have made chemistry impos-
     sible. How is it possible for the same one-force
     strength to satisfy so many different requirements,
     when it seems that different strengths would be
     required for each one of these processes?[3]

ACROSS THE MULTIVERSE

Opposed to the idea of divine design is the theory of the
multiverse. (I shall argue, however, that the existence of a

multiverse still does not eliminate the question of a divine Source.) One of the most prominent proponents of the multiverse is cosmologist Martin Rees. Rees observes:

> Any universe hospitable to life—what we might call a *biophilic universe*—has to be "adjusted" in a particular way. The prerequisites for any life of the kind we know about—long-lived stable stars, stable atoms such as carbon, oxygen and silicon, able to combine into complex molecules, etc.—are sensitive to the physical laws and to the size, expansion rate and contents of the universe.[4]

This could be explained, he says, by the hypothesis that there are many "universes" with different laws and physical constants, and ours happens to be one belonging to a subset of universes that are conducive to the appearance of complexity and consciousness. If this is the case, fine tuning would not be surprising.

Rees mentions the most influential variations of the multiverse idea. In the "eternal inflationary" idea of cosmologists Andrei Linde and Alex Vilenkin, universes emerge from individual big bangs with space-time dimensions entirely different from those of the universe we know. The black hole thesis of Alan Guth, David Harrison, and Lee Smolin holds that universes materialize from black holes in mutually inaccessible space-time domains. Finally, Lisa Randall and Raman Sundrum propose that there are universes in different spatial dimensions that may or may not interact gravitationally with each other. Rees points out that these multiverse ideas are "highly speculative" and require a theory that consistently describes the physics of ultrahigh densities, the configuration of structures on extra dimensions, and so forth. He notes that only one of them can be right. And, in fact, he adds, "Quite possibly none is: there are alternative theories that would lead just to one universe."[5]

A BLUNDERBUSS THEORY

Both Paul Davies and Richard Swinburne reject the multiverse idea. Davies, a physicist and cosmologist, writes that "it is trivially true that, in an infinite universe, anything that can happen will happen." But this is not an explanation at all. If we are trying to understand why the universe is bio-friendly, we are not helped by being told that all possible universes exist. "Like a blunderbuss, it explains everything and nothing." By this he means that it is a vacuous claim. If we say that the world and everything in it came into being five minutes ago complete with our memories of living for many years and evidence of events occurring thousands of years ago, then our claim cannot be refuted. It explains everything and yet nothing.

A true scientific explanation, says Davies, is like a single well-aimed bullet. The idea of a multiverse replaces the rationally ordered real world with an infinitely complex charade and makes the whole idea of "explanation" meaningless.[6] Swinburne is just as strong in his disdain for the multiverse explanation: "It is crazy to postulate a trillion (causally unconnected) universes to explain the features of one universe, when postulating one entity (God) will do the job."[7]

Three things might be said concerning the arguments about fine tuning. First, it is a hard fact that we live in a universe with certain laws and constants, and life would not have been possible if some of these laws and constants had been different. Second, the fact that the existing laws and constants allow the survival of life does not answer the question of the origin of life. This is a very different question, as I will try to show; these conditions are necessary for life to arise, but not sufficient. Third, the fact that it is logically possible that there are multiple universes with their own laws of nature does not show that such universes do exist. There is currently no evidence in support of a multiverse. It remains a speculative idea.

What is especially important here is the fact that the existence of a multiverse does not explain the origin of the laws of nature. Martin Rees suggests that the existence of different universes with their own laws raises the question of the laws governing the entire multiverse, the overarching theory governing the ensemble. *"The underlying laws governing the entire multiverse may allow variety among the universes,"* he writes. "Some of what we call 'laws of nature' may in this grander perspective be *local bylaws,* consistent with some overarching theory governing the ensemble, but not uniquely fixed by that theory."[8]

To ask how the laws governing the multiverse originated is the same as asking for the origin of the laws of nature in general. Paul Davies notes:

> Multiverse proponents are often vague about how the parameter values are chosen across the defined ensemble. If there is a "law of laws" describing how parameter values are assigned as one slips from one universe to the next, then we have only shifted the problem of cosmic biophilicity up one level. Why? First, because we need to explain where the law of laws comes from.[9]

Some have said that the laws of nature are simply accidental results of the way the universe cooled after the big bang. But, as Rees has pointed out, even such accidents can be regarded as secondary manifestations of deeper laws governing the ensemble of universes. Again, even the evolution of the laws of nature and changes to the constants follow certain laws. "We're still left with the question of how these 'deeper' laws originated. No matter how far you push back the properties of the universe as somehow 'emergent,' their very emergence has to follow certain prior laws."[10]

So multiverse or not, we still have to come to terms with the origin of the laws of nature. And the only viable explanation here is the divine Mind.

7

HOW DID LIFE GO LIVE?

When the mass media first reported the change in my view of the world, I was quoted as saying that biologists' investigation of DNA has shown, by the almost unbelievable complexity of the arrangements needed to produce life, that intelligence must have been involved. I had previously written that there was room for a new argument to design in explaining the first emergence of living from nonliving matter—especially where this first living matter already possessed the capacity to reproduce itself genetically. I maintained that there was no satisfactory naturalistic explanation for such a phenomenon.

These statements provoked an outcry from critics who claimed that I was not familiar with the latest work in abiogenesis. Richard Dawkins claimed that I was appealing to a "god of the gaps." In my new introduction to the 2005 edition of *God and Philosophy*, I said, "I am myself delighted to be assured by biological-scientist friends that protobiologists are now well able to produce theories of the evolution of the first living matter and that several of these theories are consistent with all the so-far-confirmed scientific evidence."[1] But to this I must add the caveat that the latest work I have seen shows that the present physicists' view of the age of the universe gives too little time for these theories of abiogenesis to get the job done.

A far more important consideration is the philosophical challenge facing origin-of-life studies. Most studies on the origin of life are carried out by scientists who rarely attend to the philosophical dimension of their findings. Philosophers, on the other hand, have said little on the nature and origin of life. The philosophical question that has not been answered in origin-of-life studies is this: How can a universe of mindless matter produce beings with intrinsic ends, self-replication capabilities, and "coded chemistry"? Here we are not dealing with biology, but an entirely different category of problem.

THE PURPOSE-DRIVEN ORGANISM

Let us first look at the nature of life from a philosophical standpoint. Living matter possesses an inherent goal or end-centered organization that is nowhere present in the matter that preceded it. In one of the few recent philosophical works on life, Richard Cameron has presented a useful analysis of this directedness of living beings.

Something that is alive, says Cameron, will also be teleological—that is, it will possess intrinsic ends, goals, or purposes. "Contemporary biologists, philosophers of biology, and workers in the field of 'artificial life,'" he writes, "have yet to produce a satisfying account of what it is to be alive, and I defend the view that Aristotle can help us fill this gap.... Aristotle did not hold life and teleology to be coextensive simply by chance, but defined life in teleological terms, holding that teleology is essential to the life of living things."[2]

The origin of self-reproduction is a second key problem. Distinguished philosopher John Haldane notes that origin-of-life theories "do not provide a sufficient explanation, since they presuppose the existence at an early stage of self-reproduction, and it has not been shown that this can arise by natural means from a material base."[3]

David Conway summarizes these two philosophical quandaries in responding to David Hume's contention that the life-sustaining order of the universe was not designed by any form of intelligence. The first challenge is to produce a materialistic explanation for "the very first emergence of living matter from non-living matter. In being alive, living matter possesses a teleological organization that is wholly absent from everything that preceded it." The second challenge is to produce an equally materialist explanation for "the emergence, from the very earliest life-forms which were incapable of reproducing themselves, of life-forms with a capacity for reproducing themselves. Without the existence of such a capacity, it would not have been possible for different species to emerge through random mutation and natural selection. Accordingly, such mechanism cannot be invoked in any explanation of how life-forms with this capacity first 'evolved' from those that lacked it." Conway concludes that these biological phenomena "provide us with reason for doubting that it is possible to account for existent life-forms in purely materialistic terms and without recourse to design."[4]

A DEEP CONCEPTUAL CHALLENGE

A third philosophical dimension to the origin of life relates to the origin of the coding and information processing that is central to all life-forms. This is well described by the mathematician David Berlinski, who points out that there is a rich narrative drama surrounding our current understanding of the cell.

The genetic message in DNA is duplicated in replication and then copied from DNA to RNA in transcription. Following this there is translation whereby the message from RNA is conveyed to the amino acids, and finally the amino acids are assembled into proteins. The cell's two fundamentally different structures of information management and chemical activity are coordinated by the universal genetic code.

The remarkable nature of this phenomenon becomes apparent when we highlight the word *code*. Berlinski writes:

> By itself, a code is familiar enough, an arbitrary mapping or a system of linkages between two discrete combinatorial objects. The Morse code, to take a familiar example, coordinates dashes and dots with letters of the alphabet. To note that codes are arbitrary is to note the distinction between a code and a purely physical connection between two objects. To note that codes embody mappings is to embed the concept of a code in mathematical language. To note that codes reflect a linkage of some sort is to return the concept of a code to its human uses.

This in turn leads to the big question: "Can the origins of a system of coded chemistry be explained in a way that makes no appeal whatever to the kinds of facts that we otherwise invoke to explain codes and languages, systems of communication, the impress of ordinary words on the world of matter?"[5]

Carl Woese, a leader in origin-of-life studies, draws attention to the philosophically puzzling nature of this phenomenon. Writing in the journal *RNA,* he says: "The coding, mechanistic, and evolutionary facets of the problem now became separate issues. The idea that gene expression, like gene replication, was underlain by some fundamental physical principle was gone." Not only is there no underlying physical principle, but the very existence of a code is a mystery. "The coding rules (the dictionary of codon assignments) are known. Yet they provide no clue as to why the code exists and why the mechanism of translation is what it is." He frankly admits that we do not know anything about the origin of such a system. "The origins of translation, that is before it became a true decoding mechanism, are for now lost in the dimness of the past, and I don't wish to engage here in hand-waving speculations as to what polymerization processes might have preceded and given rise to it, or to speculate on the origins of tRNA, tRNA charging systems or the genetic code."[6]

Paul Davies highlights the same problem. He observes that most theories of biogenesis have concentrated on the chemistry of life, but "life is more than just complex chemical reactions. The cell is also an information storing, processing and replicating system. We need to explain the origin of this information, and the way in which the information processing machinery came to exist." He emphasizes the fact that a gene is nothing but a set of coded instructions with a precise recipe for manufacturing proteins. Most important, these genetic instructions are not the kind of information you find in thermodynamics and statistical mechanics; rather, they constitute semantic information. In other words, they have a specific meaning. These instructions can be effective only in a molecular environment capable of interpreting the meaning in the genetic code. The origin question rises to the top at this point. "The problem of how meaningful or semantic information can emerge spontaneously from a collection of mindless molecules subject to blind and purposeless forces presents a deep conceptual challenge."[7]

THROUGH A GLASS DARKLY

It is true that protobiologists do have theories of the evolution of the first living matter, but they are dealing with a different category of problem. They are dealing with the interaction of chemicals, whereas our questions have to do with how something can be intrinsically purpose-driven and how matter can be managed by symbol processing. But even at their own level, the protobiologists are still a long way from any definitive conclusions. This is highlighted by two prominent origin-of-life researchers.

Andy Knoll, a professor of biology at Harvard and author of *Life on a Young Planet: The First Three Billion Years of Life*, notes:

> If we try to summarize by just saying what, at the end of the day, we do know about the deep history of life on Earth, about its origin, about its formative stages that gave rise to the biology we see around us today, I think we have to admit that we're looking through a glass darkly here. We don't know how life started on this planet. We don't know exactly when it started, we don't know under what circumstances.[8]

Antonio Lazcano, the president of the International Society for the Study of the Origin of Life, reports: "One feature of life, though, remains certain: Life could not have evolved without a genetic mechanism—one able to store, replicate, and transmit to its progeny information that can change with time.... Precisely how the first genetic machinery evolved also persists as an unresolved issue." In fact, he says, "The exact pathway for life's origin may never be known."[9]

As for the origin of reproduction, John Maddox, the editor emeritus of *Nature*, writes, "The overriding question is when (and then how) sexual reproduction itself evolved.

Despite decades of speculation, we do not know."[10] Finally, scientist Gerald Schroeder points out that the existence of conditions favorable to life still does not explain how life itself originated. Life was able to survive only because of favorable conditions on our planet. But there is no law of nature that instructs matter to produce end-directed, self-replicating entities.

So how do we account for the origin of life? The Nobel Prize–winning physiologist George Wald once famously argued that "we choose to believe the impossible: that life arose spontaneously by chance." In later years, he concluded that a preexisting mind, which he posits as the matrix of physical reality, composed a physical universe that breeds life:

How is it that, with so many other apparent options, we are in a universe that possesses just that peculiar nexus of properties that breeds life? It has occurred to me lately—I must confess with some shock at first to my scientific sensibilities—that both questions might be brought into some degree of congruence. This is with the assumption that mind, rather than emerging as a late outgrowth in the evolution of life, has existed always as the matrix, the source and condition of physical reality—that the stuff of which physical reality is constructed is mind-stuff.

It is mind that has composed a physical universe that breeds life, and so eventually evolves creatures that know and create: science-, art-, and technology-making creatures.[11]

This, too, is my conclusion. The only satisfactory explanation for the origin of such "end-directed, self-replicating" life as we see on earth is an infinitely intelligent Mind.

8

DID SOMETHING COME FROM NOTHING?

In a scene late in the movie *The Sound of Music*, Maria, played by Julie Andrews, and Captain von Trapp, played by Christopher Plummer, finally confess their love for one another. Each seems amazed to be loved by the other, and they wonder together how their love could have come about. But they seem confident it came from somewhere. In the lyrics of Richard Rodgers, they sing:

> *Nothing comes from nothing,*
> *Nothing ever could.*[1]

But is that true? Or can something come from nothing? And how does that question affect our understanding of how the universe came into being?

This is the subject matter of the scientific discipline of cosmology and of the cosmological argument in philosophy. In *The Presumption of Atheism,* I defined a cosmological argument as one that takes as its starting point the claim that there exists a universe. By universe, I meant one or more beings caused to exist by some other being (or that could be the causes of the existence of other beings).

THE ULTIMATE UNIVERSE

In *The Presumption of Atheism* and other atheistic writings, I argued that we must take the universe itself and its most fundamental laws as themselves ultimate. Every system of explanation must start somewhere, and this starting point itself cannot be explained by the system. So, inevitably, all such systems include at least some fundamentals that are not themselves explained. This is a consequence following from the essential nature of explanations of why something that is in fact the case, is the case.

Suppose, for instance, that we notice that the new white paint above our gas stove has turned a dirty brown. We investigate. We discover that this is what always happens with that sort of stove and that kind of paint. Pressing our questioning to a second stage, we learn that this phenomenon is to be explained by certain wider and deeper regularities of chemical combination: the sulfur in the gas fumes forms a compound with something in the paint, and that is what changes its color. Driving on still further, we are led to see the squalor in our kitchen as one of the innumerable consequences of the truth of an all-embracing atomic-molecular theory of the structure of matter. And so it goes. At every stage, the explanation has to assume some things as brute facts; that is just how things are.

In debating those who believed in God, I showed that they faced this same inevitability. Whatever else theists may think to explain by reference to the existence and nature of their God, they cannot avoid taking that fact as ultimate and beyond explanation. And I did not see how anything within our universe can be either known or reasonably conjectured to be pointing to some transcendent reality behind, above, or beyond. So why not take the universe and its most fundamental features as the ultimate fact?

Now, most of my above discussions were carried on independent of developments in modern cosmology. In fact, my two main antitheological books were both written long before either the development of the big-bang cosmology or the introduction of the fine-tuning argument from physical constants. But since the early 1980s, I had begun to reconsider. I confessed at that point that atheists have to be embarrassed by the contemporary cosmological consensus, for it seemed that the cosmologists were providing a scientific proof of what St. Thomas Aquinas contended could not be proved philosophically; namely, that the universe had a beginning.

IN THE BEGINNING

When I first met the big-bang theory as an atheist, it seemed to me the theory made a big difference because it suggested that the universe had a beginning and that the first sentence in Genesis ("In the beginning, God created the heavens and the earth") was related to an event in the universe. As long as the universe could be comfortably thought to be not only without end but also without beginning, it remained easy to see its existence (and its most fundamental features) as brute facts. And if there had been no reason to think the universe had a beginning, there would be no need to postulate something else that produced the whole thing.

But the big-bang theory changed all that. If the universe had a beginning, it became entirely sensible, almost inevitable, to ask what produced this beginning. This radically altered the situation.

At the same time, I predicted that atheists were bound to see the big-bang cosmology as requiring a physical explanation—an explanation that, admittedly, may be forever inaccessible to human beings. But I admitted that believers could, equally reasonably, welcome the big-bang cosmology as tending to confirm their prior belief that "in the beginning" the universe was created by God.

Modern cosmologists seemed just as disturbed as atheists about the potential theological implications of their work. Consequently, they devised influential escape routes that sought to preserve the nontheist status quo. These routes included the idea of the multiverse, numerous universes generated by endless vacuum fluctuation events, and Stephen Hawking's notion of a self-contained universe.

UNTIL A BEGINNING COMES ALONG

As I have already mentioned, I did not find the multiverse alternative very helpful. The postulation of multiple universes, I maintained, is a truly desperate alternative. If the existence of one universe requires an explanation, multiple universes require a much bigger explanation: the problem is increased by the factor of whatever the total number of universes is. It seems a little like the case of a schoolboy whose teacher doesn't believe his dog ate his homework, so he replaces the first version with the story that a pack of dogs—too many to count—ate his homework.

Stephen Hawking took a different approach in his book *A Brief History of Time*. He wrote: "So long as the universe had a beginning, we could suppose it had a creator. But if the universe is really self-contained, having no boundary or edge, it would have neither beginning nor end, it would simply be. What place, then, for a creator?"[2] In reviewing the book when it came out, I pointed out that the suggestion embodied in that concluding rhetorical question could not help but appeal to the ungodly. Yet, however congenial that conclusion, I added, anyone who is not a theoretical physicist is bound to be tempted to respond, like some character from Damon Runyon's Broadway: "If the big bang was not a beginning, still it will at least do until a beginning comes along."[3] Hawking himself must have at least some sympathy with such a response, for he said, "An expanding universe does not preclude a creator, but it does place limits on when he might have carried out his job!"

Hawking had also said, "One may say that time had a beginning at the big bang, in the sense that earlier times simply would not be defined."[4] I concluded from this discussion that, even if it were agreed that the universe as we know it began with the big bang, physics must nonetheless remain radically agnostic: it is physically impossible to discover what, if anything, caused that big bang.

Certainly the revelation of a universe in flux as opposed to a static eternally inert entity made a difference to the discussion. But the moral of the story was that, ultimately, the issues at stake were philosophical rather than scientific. And this brought me back to the cosmological argument.

SOMETHING TOO BIG FOR SCIENCE TO EXPLAIN

The primary philosophical critic of the cosmological argument for God's existence was David Hume. Although I had endorsed Hume's arguments in my earlier books, I had begun to express misgivings about his methodology. For instance, I had pointed out in an essay, in a festschrift for the philosopher Terence Penelhum, that certain presuppositions of Hume's thinking resulted in crucial errors. This included his thesis that what we call "causes" are nothing more than a matter of associations of ideas or lack of such associations. I said that the origin of—or at least the validation for—our causal concepts, the grounds upon which our causal knowledge has to be based, lie in our abundant and ever repeated experience of activity as creatures of flesh and blood operating in a mind-independent world (experience, that is, of trying to push or pull things about and of succeeding in pushing or pulling some but not others; experience of wondering "what would happen if," of experimenting, and thus of discovering through experiment "what does happen when"). It is as agents that we acquire, apply, and validate the idea of cause and effect and its component notion of what is necessary and what is impossible. I concluded that a purely Humean story could not compass the established meanings of "cause" and of "law of nature."[5]

But in David Conway's *The Rediscovery of Wisdom* and the 2004 edition of Richard Swinburne's *The Existence of God*, I found especially effective responses to the Humean (and Kantian) critique of the cosmological argument. Conway systematically addresses each of Hume's objections. For instance, Hume held that there is no cause of the existence of any series of physical beings beyond the sum of each member of the series. If there is a beginningless series of nonnecessary existent beings, then this is a sufficient cause for the universe as a whole. Conway rejected this objection on the grounds that "the causal explanations of the parts of any such whole in terms of other parts cannot add up to a causal explanation of the whole, if the items mentioned as causes are items whose own existence stands in need of a causal explanation."[6] So, for example, consider a software virus capable of replicating itself on computers connected by a network. The fact that a million computers have been infected by the virus does not in itself explain the existence of the self-replicating virus.

Concerning the same Humean argument, Swinburne said:

The whole infinite series will have no explanation at all, for there will be no causes of members of the series lying outside the series. In that case, the existence of the universe over infinite time will be an inexplicable brute fact. There will be an explanation (in terms of laws) of why, once existent, it continues to exist. But what will be inexplicable is its existence at all throughout infinite time. The existence of a complex physical universe over finite or infinite time is something "too big" for science to explain.[7]

THE NEED FOR A CREATIVE FACTOR

Once the Humean critique has been met, it is possible to apply the cosmological argument in the context of modern cosmology. Swinburne argues that we can explain states of affairs only in terms of other states of affairs. Laws by themselves cannot explain these states. "We need states of affairs as well as laws to explain things," he writes. "And if we do not have them for the beginning of the universe, because there are no earlier states, then we cannot explain the beginning of the universe."[8] If there is to be a plausible law to explain the beginning of the universe, then it would have to say something like "empty space necessarily gives rise to matter-energy." Here "empty space" is not nothing, but rather an "identifiable particular," a something that is already there. This reliance on laws to get the universe started from "empty space" also raises the question of why matter-energy was produced at time t° rather than at some other time.

The philosopher of science John Leslie has shown that none of today's fashionable cosmological speculations preclude the possibility of a Creator. A number of cosmologists have speculated that the universe emerged from "nothing." Edward Tryon, in 1973, had theorized that the universe was a fluctuation in the vacuum of a larger space. He argued that the total energy of the universe was zero because the gravitational binding energy of the universe is shown as a negative quantity in physicists' equations. Using another approach, Jim Hartle, Stephen Hawking, and Alex Vilenkin have speculated that the universe quantum-fluctuated into existence "from nothing." The "nothing" is in certain instances a chaotic space-time foam with fantastically high energy density. Another suggestion (from Hawking) is that "time becomes more and more space-like at earlier and earlier moments in the big bang."

Leslie does not think these speculations are relevant because, he says:

> No matter how you describe the universe—as having existed for ever, or as having originated from a point outside space-time or else in space but not in time, or as starting off so quantum-fuzzily that there was no definite point at which it started, or as

having a total energy that is zero—the people who see a problem in the sheer existence of Something Rather Than Nothing will be little inclined to agree that the problem has been solved.[9]

If you had an equation detailing the probability of something emerging from a vacuum, you would still have to ask why that equation applies. Hawking had, in fact, noted the need for a creative factor to breathe fire into the equations.

In an interview soon after the publication of *A Brief History of Time*, Hawking acknowledged that his model did not have any bearing on the existence of God. In saying that the laws of physics determined how the universe began, we are only saying that God did not choose "to set the universe going in some arbitrary way that we couldn't understand. It says nothing about whether or not God exists—just that He is not arbitrary."[10]

A GOOD C-INDUCTIVE ARGUMENT

The old attempt to explain the universe by reference to an infinite series of causes has been recast in the language of modern cosmology. But John Leslie finds this unsatisfactory. Some people, he remarks, claim that the existence of the universe at any given moment can be explained by the fact that it existed at an earlier moment and so on, ad infinitum. Then there are physicists who believe that the universe existed over infinite time either through an infinite series of bangs and crunches or as part of an eternally expanding reality that produces new big-bang universes. Yet others say the universe existed from a finite past by one way of measuring, but over infinite time by another measure.

In response to these approaches, Leslie asserts that "the existence even of an infinite series of past events couldn't be made self-explaining through each even being explained by an earlier one." If there is an infinite series of books about geometry that owe their pattern to copying from earlier books, we still do not have an adequate answer as to why the book is the way it is (e.g., it is about geometry) or why there is a book at all. The entire series needs an explanation. "Think of a time machine," he writes, "that travels into the past so that nobody need ever have designed and manufactured it. Its existence forms a self-explaining temporal loop! Even if time travel made sense, this would surely be nonsense."[11]

Richard Swinburne summarizes his exposition of the cosmological argument by saying: "There is quite a chance that, if there is a God, he will make something of the finitude and complexity of a universe. It is very unlikely that a universe would exist uncaused, but rather more likely that God would exist uncaused. Hence the argument from the existence of the universe to the existence of God is a good C-inductive argument."[12] In a recent discussion with Swinburne, I noted that his version of the cosmological argument seems to be right in a fundamental way. Some features of it may need to be amended, but the universe is something that begs an explanation. Richard Swinburne's cosmological argument provides a very promising explanation, probably the finally right one.

9

FINDING SPACE
FOR GOD

It is the stuff of Shakespeare. In the first act of *Macbeth*, one of Shakespeare's most famous plays, Macbeth and Banquo, two generals in the king's army, encounter a trio of witches. The witches speak to them and then disappear.

An amazed Banquo says, "The earth hath bubbles, as the water has, and these are of them. Whither are they vanished?"

"Into the air," answers Macbeth. "And what seem'd corporal melted as breath into the wind."

It is entertaining theater, and fine literature. But although the idea of a person who can melt "as breath into the wind" seldom presents a problem for fans of theater and literature, it has in the past posed quite an obstacle for this philosopher seeking to "follow the evidence wherever it may lead."

THERE'S NO ONE THERE

In *God and Philosophy* and later publications, I argued that the concept of God was not coherent because it presupposed the idea of an incorporeal omnipresent Spirit. My rationale was fairly straightforward. As we understand it in ordinary meanings and corresponding usage, a person is a creature of flesh and blood. In this respect, the expression "person without a body" seemed nonsensical, like the little rhyme credited to Hughes Mearns:

> *As I was walking up the stair*
> *I met a man who wasn't there.*
> *He wasn't there again today.*
> *Oh, how I wish he'd go away.*

To say "person without a body" is much like saying "someone who isn't there." If we want to speak of "person without a body," we shall need to provide some appropriate means of identifying and reidentifying the person in some new sense of the word "person."

Later philosophers such as Peter Strawson and Bede Rundle have continued to develop this critique. Most recently, we find a version of this argument in the work of John Gaskin, a professor of philosophy and fellow of Trinity College, Dublin. He writes: "The absence of a body is therefore not only factual grounds for doubting whether a person exists (there's no one there!). It is also grounds for doubting whether such a bodiless entity could possibly be an agent."[1]

Although formidable, this critique has been credibly addressed by theists. Since the 1980s and 1990s, there has been a renaissance of theism among analytic philosophers. Many of these thinkers have done extensive studies on the attributes traditionally attributed to God and on such concepts as eternity. Two such thinkers, Thomas Tracy and Brian Leftow, have systematically responded to the challenge of defending the coherence of the idea of an "incorporeal omnipresent Spirit." While Tracy addresses the question of how a bodiless agent can be identified, Leftow attempts to show both why a divine being must be outside space and time and how a bodiless being can act in the universe.

THE PERFECTION OF AGENCY

In his books *God, Action and Embodiment* and *The God Who Acts,* Tracy has extensively answered my questions of how it is possible for there to be a person without a body and how such a person could be identified. Tracy considers persons (human and divine) to be agents that can act intentionally. He sees the human person as an agent organism, a body capable of intentional action. But though all embodied agents (such as human persons) must be psychophysical units (and not minds plus bodies), all agents do not have to be embodied. No antidualist argument shows that a body is a necessary condition for being an agent, since the condition for being an agent is simply to be capable of intentional action. God is an agent, he notes, whose every activity is intentional action. To speak of God as a personal being is to talk of him as an agent of intentional actions. God's powers of action are unique, and the actions ascribed to God cannot in principle be attributed to other agents. For instance, God, through his intentional agency, is the agent who brings into existence all other beings.

Tracy observes that God can be identified through the unique mode in which he acts. "If we conceive of God as the perfection of agency, then we will say that God is a radically self-creative agent whose life displays a perfect unity of intention and who is the omnipotent creator of all things." To say that God is loving is to say that God loves in concrete ways, shown in his actions, and these actions represent his identity as an agent. But God is an agent whose mode of life and powers of action are fundamentally different from ours. Since "the scope and content of God's action is unique, then so too will be the character of his love or patience or wisdom."[2] Such apprehension of divine actions can help give content to our descriptions of God as loving or wise, but we still have to admit that our understanding is radically limited.

THE REAL FURNITURE OF THE WORLD

Brian Leftow, currently Nolloth Professor at Oxford, treats these themes in his book *Time and Eternity*. In my discussion with him, Leftow pointed out that the idea of God being outside space and time is consistent with the theory of special relativity. "There are a lot of different arguments you might give to try and show that God is outside time," he noted. "One that impresses me somewhat is simply that if you take special relativity very seriously, you believe that everything that is in time is also in space. It's just a four-dimensional continuum. No theist has ever thought that God was literally there in space. If he's not in space and whatever is in time is in space, then he is not in time. The question then becomes: What sense can you make out of there being a personlike being outside of time?"

Leftow continued:

Well, obviously, a lot of personal predicates won't apply. He can't forget. You can only forget what's in your past. He can't cease to do something. You can only cease to do something that's over in your past. But there are other personal predicates that don't seem to make an essential reference to time—things like knowing, which can just be a dispositional state without a temporal reference. And, I would argue, intending as well. Having an intention can be a dispositional state such that if certain things were to occur you would do something. So I'm inclined to think that there are reasons to think that God is outside time. And also that we can make some sense that doesn't drive us into a mystery muddle.

The other question he addressed was how it makes sense to talk of an omnipresent Spirit acting in space or in the world:

If God is timeless, then everything he does, he does, so to speak, all at once, in a single act. He couldn't do one thing first and then another later on. But that one act might have effects at different times. He might in one volition will that the sun rise today and the sun rise tomorrow and this has effects today and tomorrow. That, however, is not the most basic question.

The most basic question is: How could there be a causal connection between a spaceless, timeless being and the entirety of space-time? Whether you can make sense of that depends very much on what your theory of causation is. If you think that the concept of cause involves an essential temporal reference [i.e., that cause is tied to time]—for example, a cause is an event that precedes another event and has certain other relations to it—then that's going to be ruled out. But there are analyses of cause that don't involve that essential temporal reference. I myself am inclined to the view that the concept of cause doesn't really have an analysis—that it's just a primitive concept and that causation itself is a primitive relation. It's part of the real furniture of the world. If the concept of cause doesn't have an analysis, then there isn't anything you can pull out of it by way of an analysis that would rule out a primitive causal connection between a nontemporal God and the whole of time.[3]

A COHERENT POSSIBILITY

At the very least, the studies of Tracy and Leftow show that the idea of an omnipresent Spirit is not intrinsically incoherent if we see such a Spirit as an agent outside space and time that uniquely executes its intentions in the spatio-temporal continuum. The question of whether such a Spirit exists, as we have seen, lies at the heart of the arguments for God's existence.

As to the validity of these arguments, I concur with Conway's conclusion:

> If the reasoning of the preceding chapter has been sound, there are no good philosophical arguments for denying God to be the explanation of the universe and of the form of order it exhibits. This being so, there is no good reason for philosophers not to return once more to the classical conception of their subject, provided there are no better ways to obtain wisdom.[4]

10

OPEN TO OMNIPOTENCE

Science qua science cannot furnish an argument for God's existence. But the three items of evidence we have considered in this volume—the laws of nature, life with its teleological organization, and the existence of the universe—can only be explained in the light of an Intelligence that explains both its own existence and that of the world. Such a discovery of the Divine does not come through experiments and equations, but through an understanding of the structures they unveil and map.

Now, all this might sound abstract and impersonal. How, it might be asked, do I as a person respond to the discovery of an ultimate Reality that is an omnipresent and omniscient Spirit? I must say again that the journey to my discovery of the Divine has thus far been a pilgrimage of reason. I have followed the argument where it has led me. And it has led me to accept the existence of a self-existent, immutable, immaterial, omnipotent, and omniscient Being.

Certainly, the existence of evil and suffering must be faced. However, philosophically speaking, that is a separate issue from the question of God's existence. From the existence of nature, we arrive at the ground of its existence. Nature may have its imperfections, but this says nothing as to whether it had an ultimate Source. Thus, the existence of God does not depend on the existence of warranted or unwarranted evil.

With regard to explaining the presence of evil, there are two alternate explanations for those who accept the existence of the Divine. The first is that of the Aristotelian God who does not intervene in the world. The second is the free-will defense, the idea that evil is always a possibility if human beings are truly free. In the Aristotelian framework, once the work of creation is completed, God leaves the universe subject to the laws of nature, although perhaps sometimes providing a rather distant and detached endorsement of the fundamental principles of justice. The free-will defense depends on the prior acceptance of a framework of divine revelation, the idea that God has revealed himself.

OPEN TO LEARNING MORE

Where do I go from here? In the first place, I am entirely open to learning more about the divine Reality, especially in the light of what we know about the history of nature. Second, the question of whether the Divine has revealed itself in human history remains a valid topic of discussion. You cannot limit the possibilities of omnipotence except to produce the logically impossible. Everything else is open to omnipotence.

Appendix B in this volume is an account of my dialogue on this latter theme with the biblical scholar and Anglican bishop N. T. Wright, with particular reference to the Christian claim that God became man in the person of Jesus Christ. As I have said more than once, no other religion enjoys anything like the combination of a charismatic figure like Jesus and a first-class intellectual like St. Paul. If you're wanting omnipotence to set up a religion, it seems to me that this is the one to beat!

WILLING TO CONNECT

I want to return now to the parable with which I began this part. We talked of the satellite phone discovered by the island tribe and the attempts to explain its nature. The parable ended with the tribal sage being ridiculed and ignored by the scientists.

But let's imagine it ending differently. The scientists adopt as a working hypothesis the sage's suggestion that the phone is a medium of contact with other humans. After further study, they confirm the conclusion that the phone is connected to a network that transmits the voices of real people. They now accept the theory that intelligent beings exist "out there."

Some of the more intrepid scientists go even farther. They work to decipher the sounds they hear on the phone. They recognize patterns and rhythms that enable them to understand what is being said. Their whole world changes. They know they are not alone. And at a certain point they make contact.

The analogy is easy to apply. The discovery of phenomena like the laws of nature—the communications network of the parable—has led scientists, philosophers, and others to accept the existence of an infinitely intelligent Mind. Some claim to have made contact with this Mind. I have not—yet. But who knows what could happen next?

Someday I might hear a Voice that says, "Can you hear me now?"

APPENDICES

In this book I have outlined the arguments that led me to change my mind about the existence of God. As noted earlier, David Conway's *The Rediscovery of Wisdom* played a significant role in that change. Another book I have recommended in other forums is *The Wonder of the World* by Roy Abraham Varghese. In my new introduction to *God and Philosophy* I said that any successor to *God and Philosophy* "would need to take into account" *The Wonder of the World,* "which provides an extremely extensive argument of the inductive argument from the order of nature." Since Varghese has collaborated with me in the production of the present book, I have asked him to supplement my reflections with an analysis and assessment of the arguments of the current generation of atheists. His paper, entitled "The 'New Atheism': A Critical Appraisal of Dawkins, Dennett, Wolpert, Harris, and Stenger," constitutes Appendix A.

Appendix B concerns the claim that there is a self-revelation of God in human history in the person of Jesus Christ. The claim is defended by one of today's premier New Testament scholars, Bishop N. T. Wright. In my view,

Wright's responses to my previous critiques of divine self-revelation, both in the present volume and in his books, comprise the most powerful case for Christianity that I have ever seen.

I included both appendices in this book because they are both examples of the kind of reasoning that led me to change my mind about God's existence. I felt it appropriate to include them in their entirety because they are original contributions that advance the discussion significantly while also giving readers some insight into the direction of my continuing journey. When taken in conjunction with Part II, "My Discovery of the Divine," they constitute an organic whole that provides a powerful new vision of the philosophy of religion.

APPENDIX A

The "New Atheism":
A Critical Appraisal of Dawkins, Dennett,
Wolpert, Harris, and Stenger

Roy Abraham Varghese

At the foundation of the "new atheism" is the belief that there is no God, no eternal and infinite Source of all that exists. This is the key belief that needs to be established in order for most of the other arguments to work. It is my contention here that the "new atheists," Richard Dawkins, Daniel Dennett, Lewis Wolpert, Sam Harris, and Victor Stenger, not only fail to make a case for this belief, but ignore the very phenomena that are particularly relevant to the question of whether God exists.

As I see it, five phenomena are evident in our immediate experience that can only be explained in terms of the existence of God. These are, first, the rationality implicit in all our experience of the physical world; second, life, the capacity to act autonomously; third, consciousness, the ability to be aware; fourth, conceptual thought, the power of articulating and understanding meaningful symbols such as are embedded in language; and, fifth, the human self, the "center" of consciousness, thought, and action.

Three things should be said about these phenomena and their application to the existence of God. First, we are accustomed to hearing about arguments and proofs for God's existence. In my view, such arguments are useful in articulating certain fundamental insights, but cannot be regarded as "proofs" whose formal validity determines whether there is a God. Rather, each of the five phenomena adduced here, in their own way, presuppose the existence of an infinite, eternal Mind. God is the condition that underlies all that is self-evident in our experience. Second, as should be obvious from the previous point, we are not talking about probabilities and hypotheses, but about encounters with fundamental realities that cannot be denied without self-contradiction. In other words, we don't apply probability theorems to certain sets of data, but consider the far more basic question of how it is possible to evaluate data at all. Equally, it is not a matter of deducing God from the existence of certain complex phenomena. Rather, God's existence is presupposed by all phenomena. Third, atheists, new and old, have complained that there is no evidence for God's existence, and some theists have responded that our free will can be preserved only if such evidence is nonco-

ercive. The approach taken here is that we have all the evidence we need in our immediate experience and that only
a deliberate refusal to "look" is responsible for atheism of
any variety.

In considering our immediate experience, let us perform a thought experiment. Think for a minute of a marble table in front of you. Do you think that, given a trillion
years or infinite time, this table could suddenly or gradu-
ally become conscious, aware of its surroundings, aware
of its identity the way you are? It is simply inconceivable
that this would or could happen. And the same goes for
any kind of matter. Once you understand the nature of
matter, of mass-energy, you realize that, by its very nature,
it could never become "aware," never "think," never say
"I." But the atheist position is that, at some point in the
history of the universe, the impossible and the inconceivable took place. Undifferentiated matter (here we include
energy), at some point, became "alive," then conscious,
then conceptually proficient, then an "I." But returning to
our table, we see why this is simply laughable. The table
has none of the properties of being conscious and, given
infinite time, it cannot "acquire" such properties. Even
if one subscribes to some far-fetched scenario of the origin of life, one would have take leave of one's senses to
suggest that, given certain conditions, a piece of marble
could produce concepts. And, at a subatomic level, what

holds for the table holds for all the other matter in the universe.

Over the last three hundred years, empirical science has uncovered immeasurably more data about the physical world than could ever have been imagined by our ancestors. This includes a comprehensive understanding of the genetic and neural networks that underlie life, consciousness, thought, and the self. But beyond saying that these four phenomena operate with a physical infrastructure that is better understood than ever before, science cannot say anything about the nature or origin of the phenomena themselves. Although individual scientists have tried to explain them as manifestations of matter, there is no way possible to demonstrate that my understanding of this sentence is nothing but a specific neural transaction. Granted, there are neural transactions that accompany my thoughts—and modern neuroscience has pinpointed the regions of the brain that support different kinds of mental activity. But to say that a given thought *is* one specific neural transaction set is as inane as suggesting that the idea of justice is nothing but certain marks of ink on paper. It is incoherent, then, to suggest that consciousness and thought are simply and solely physical transactions.

Given the limited space here, I present an extremely condensed overview of the five fundamental phenomena that underlie our experience of the world and that cannot be explained within the framework of the "new atheism." A more detailed study will be found in my forthcoming book *The Missing Link.*

RATIONALITY

Dawkins and the others ask, "Who created God?" Now, clearly, theists and atheists can agree on one thing: if anything at all exists, there must be something preceding it that always existed. How did this eternally existing reality come to be? The answer is that it never came to be. It always existed. Take your pick: God or universe. Something always existed.

It is precisely at this point that the theme of rationality returns to the forefront. Contrary to the protestations of the atheists, there is a major difference between what theists and atheists claim about that which always exists. Atheists say that the explanation for the universe is simply that it is eternally existing, but we cannot explain how this eternally existing state of affairs came to be. It is inexplicable and has to be accepted as such. Theists, however, are adamant in pointing out that God is something that is not ultimately inexplicable: God's existence is inexplicable to us, but not to God.

That God's eternal existence has to have its own inner logic we can see, because there can be rationality in the universe only if it is grounded in ultimate rationality. In other words, such singular facts as our capacity to know and explicate truths, the correlation between the workings of nature and our abstract descriptions of these workings (what physicist Eugene Wigner called the unreasonable effectiveness of mathematics), and the role of codes (systems of symbols that act in the physical world) such as the genetic and neuronal codes at the most fundamental levels of life manifest by their very being the foundational and all-pervasive nature of rationality. *What* this inner logic is we cannot see, although traditional ideas about the nature of God certainly give some hints. For instance, Eleonore Stump and Norman Kretzmann have argued that the divine attribute of absolute simplicity, when fully understood, helps show why God cannot not exist. Alvin Plantinga points out that God understood as a necessary Being exists in all possible worlds.

Atheists may respond in two ways: the universe might have an inner logic for its existence that we cannot see; and/or we don't need to believe that there has to be a Being (God) with its own inner logic for existing. On the first point, theists will say there is no such thing as a "universe" that exists beyond the sum total of the things that constitute it, and we know for a fact that none of the things in the universe have any inner logic of unending existence. On the second, theists are simply pointing out that the existence of the rationality that we unmistakably experience—ranging from the laws of nature to our capacity for rational thought—cannot be explained if it does not have an ultimate ground, which can be nothing less than an infinite Mind. "The world is rational," noted the great mathematician Kurt Gödel.[1] The relevance of this rationality is that "the order of the world reflects the order of the supreme mind governing it."[2] The reality of rationality cannot be evaded with any appeal to natural selection. Natural selection presupposes the existence of physical entities that interact according to specific laws and of a code that manages the processes of life. And to talk of natural selection is to assume that there is some logic to what is happening in nature (adaptation) and that we are capable of understanding this logic.

Returning to the earlier example of the marble table, we are saying that the very real rationality that underlies our thinking and that we encounter in our study of a mathematically precise universe could not have been generated by a rock. God is not an ultimate brute fact, but the ultimate Rationality that is embedded in every dimension of being.

A new, albeit implausible, twist to the question of the origin of physical reality is Daniel Dennett's claim that the universe "creates itself ex nihilo, or at any rate out of something that is well-nigh indistinguishable from nothing at all."[3] This idea has been presented most clearly by another new atheist, the physicist Victor Stenger, who presents his own solution to the origins of the universe and the laws of nature in *Not by Design: The Origin of the Universe, Has Science Found God?*, *The Comprehensible Cosmos,* and *God: The Failed Hypothesis.*

Among other things, Stenger offers a novel critique of the idea of the laws of nature and their supposed implications. In *The Comprehensible Cosmos,* he holds that these so-called laws are neither handed down from above nor built-in restrictions on the behavior of matter. They are simply restrictions on the way physicists can formulate their mathematical statements about observations. Stenger's case is built on his interpretation of a key idea in modern physics, that of symmetry. According to most accounts of modern physics, *symmetry* is any kind of transformation that leaves the laws of physics that apply to a system unchanged. The idea was initially applied to the differential equations of classical mechanics and electromagnetism and then applied in new ways to special relativity and the problems of quantum mechanics. Stenger gives his readers an overview of this powerful concept, but then proceeds to draw two incoherent conclusions. One is that symmetry principles eliminate the idea of laws of nature, and the other is that nothing can produce something because "nothing" is unstable!

Amazingly, *Fearful Symmetry*, a book by Anthony Zee, a leading authority on symmetries, uses the very same facts adduced by Stenger to reach a very different conclusion:

> Symmetries have played an increasingly central role in our understanding of the physical world.... Fundamental physicists are sustained by the faith that the ultimate design is suffused with symmetries. Contemporary physics would not have been possible without symmetries to guide us.... As physics moves further away from everyday experience and closer to the mind of the Ultimate Designer, our minds are trained away from their familiar moorings.... I like to think of an Ultimate Designer defined by Symmetry, a *Deus Congruentiae*.[4]

Stenger argues that "nothing" is perfectly symmetrical because there is no absolute position, time, velocity, or acceleration in the void. The response to the question, "Where did the symmetries come from?" he says, is that they are exactly the symmetries of the void, because the laws of physics are just what they would be expected to be if they came from nothing.

Stenger's fundamental fallacy is an old one: it is the error of treating "nothing" as a kind of "something." Over the centuries, thinkers who have considered the concept of "nothing" have been careful to emphasize the point that "nothing" is not a kind of something. Absolute nothingness means no laws, no vacuums, no fields, no energy, no structures, no physical or mental entities of any kind—and no "symmetries." It has no properties or potentialities. Absolute nothingness cannot produce something given endless time—in fact, there can be no time in absolute nothingness.

What about Stenger's idea, fundamental to his book *God: The Failed Hypothesis,* that the emergence of the universe from "nothing" does not violate the principles of physics, because the net energy of the universe is zero? This is an idea first floated by the physicist Edward Tryon, who said he had shown that the net energy of the universe is almost zero and that there is therefore no contradiction in saying that it came to be out of nothing since it is nothing. If you add up the binding (attractive) energy of gravitational attraction, which is negative, and the rest of the whole mass of the universe, which is positive, you get almost zero. No energy, then, would be required to create the universe, and therefore no creator is required.

Regarding this and similar claims, the atheist philosopher J. J. C. Smart points out that the postulation of a universe with zero net energy still doesn't answer the question of why there should be anything at all. Smart notes that the hypothesis and its modern formulations still assume a structured space-time, the quantum field, and laws of nature. Consequently, they neither address the question of why anything exists nor confront the question of whether there is an atemporal cause of the space-time universe.[5]

It is apparent from this analysis that Stenger leaves two fundamental questions unanswered: Why is there something and not absolute nothingness? And why does the something that exists conform to symmetries or form complex structures?

Zee deploys the same facts of symmetry referred to by Stenger to reach the conclusion that the Mind of the ultimate Designer is the source of symmetry. The laws of nature, in fact, reflect underlying symmetries in nature. And it is symmetry, not simply the laws of nature, that points to the rationality and intelligibility of the cosmos—a rationality rooted in the Mind of God.

LIFE

The next phenomenon to be considered is life. In view of Tony Flew's treatment of the matter in this volume, not much more needs to be said here on the question of the origin of life. It should be pointed out, however, that current discussions on the question don't seem to even be aware of the key issues. There are four dimensions of living beings. Such beings are agents, goal seekers, and self-replicators, and fourthly, they are semiotically driven (their existence depends on the interplay between codes and chemistry). Each and every living being acts or is capable of action. And each such being is the unified source and center of all its actions. Since these agents are capable of surviving and acting independently, their actions are in some fashion driven by goals (nourishment), and they can reproduce themselves; they are therefore goal-seeking, self-replicating autonomous agents. Moreover, as Howard H. Pattee points out, you find in living beings the interaction of semiotic processes (rules, codes, languages, information, control) and physical systems (laws, dynamics, energy, forces, matter).[6]

Of the books under study here, only Dawkins's addresses the question of the origin of life. Wolpert is quite candid on the state of the field: "This is not to say that all the scientific questions relating to evolution have been solved. On the contrary, the origin of life itself, the evolution of the miraculous cell from which all living things evolved, is still poorly understood."[7] Dennett in previous works has simply taken it for granted that some materialist account must be right.

Unfortunately, on even the physico-chemical level, Dawkins's approach is manifestly inadequate or worse. "But how does life get started?" he asks. "The origin of life was the chemical event, or series of events, whereby the vital conditions for natural selection first came about.... Once the vital ingredient—some kind of genetic molecule—is in place, true Darwinian natural selection can follow."[8] How did this happen? "Scientists invoke the magic of large numbers.... The beauty of the anthropic principle is that it tells us, against all intuition, that a chemical model need only predict that life will arise on one planet in a billion billion to give us a good and entirely satisfying explanation for the presence of life here."[9]

Given this type of reasoning, which is better described as an audacious exercise in superstition, anything we desire should exist somewhere if we just "invoke the magic of large numbers." Unicorns or the elixir of youth, even if "staggeringly improbable," are bound to occur "against all intuition." The only requirement is "a chemical model" that "need only predict" these occurring "on one planet in a billion billion."

CONSCIOUSNESS

Fortunately, things are not quite as bad in consciousness studies. There is today a growing awareness of awareness.

We are conscious, and conscious that we are conscious. No one can deny this without self-contradiction—although some persist in doing so. The problem becomes insoluble when you realize the nature of neurons. First of all, neurons show no resemblance to our conscious life. Second and more important, their physical properties do not in any way give reason to believe that they can or will produce consciousness. Consciousness is correlated with certain regions of the brain, but when the same systems of neurons are present in the brain stem there is no "production" of consciousness. As a matter of fact, as physicist Gerald Schroeder points out, there is no essential difference in the ultimate physical constituents of a heap of sand and the brain of an Einstein. Only blind and baseless faith in matter lies behind the claim that certain bits of matter can suddenly "create" a new reality that bears no resemblance to matter.

Although mainstream body-mind studies today acknowledge the reality and consequent mystery of consciousness, Daniel Dennett is one of the few remaining philosophers who continue to evade the obvious. He says that the question of whether something is "really conscious" is not interesting or answerable and affirms that machines can be conscious because we are machines that are conscious!

Functionalism, Dennett's "explanation" for consciousness, says we should not be concerned with what makes up so-called mental phenomena. Rather, we should be investigating the functions performed by these phenomena. A pain is something that creates an avoidance reaction; a thought is an exercise in problem solving. Neither is to be thought of as a private event taking place in some private place. Ditto with all other supposedly mental phenomena. Being conscious means performing these functions. Since these functions can be replicated by nonliving systems (e.g., a computer solves problems), there is nothing mysterious about "consciousness." And certainly there's no reason to go beyond the physical.

But what this account leaves out is the fact that all mental actions are accompanied by conscious states, states in which we are aware of what we are doing. In no way does functionalism explain or claim to explain the state of being conscious, of being aware, of knowing what we are thinking about (computers don't "know" what they are doing). Still less does it tell us who it is that is conscious, aware, and thinking. Dennett, amusingly, says that the foundation of his philosophy is "third-person absolutism," which leaves him in the position of affirming, "I don't believe in 'I.'"

Interestingly, some of the strongest critics of Dennett and functionalism are themselves physicalists—David Papineau, John Searle, and others. John Searle is especially sharp: "If you are tempted to functionalism, I believe you do not need refutation, you need help."[10]

In contrast to Dennett, Sam Harris has strongly defended the supraphysical reality of consciousness. "The problem, however, is that nothing about a brain, when surveyed as a physical system, declares it to be a bearer of that peculiar, interior dimension that each of us experiences as consciousness in his own case." The upshot is startling: "Consciousness may be a far more rudimentary phenomenon than are living creatures and their brains. And there appears to be no obvious way of ruling out such a thesis experimentally."[11]

To his credit, Dawkins acknowledges the reality of both consciousness and language and the problem this poses. "Neither Steve Pinker nor I can explain human subjective consciousness—what philosophers call qualia," he said once. "In *How the Mind Works* Steve elegantly sets out the problem of subjective consciousness, and asks where it comes from and what's the explanation. Then he's honest enough to say, 'Beats the heck out of me.' That is an honest thing to say, and I echo it. We don't know. We don't understand it."[12] Wolpert deliberately avoids the entire issue of consciousness—"I have purposely avoided any discussion of consciousness."[13]

THOUGHT

Beyond consciousness, there is the phenomenon of thought, of understanding, seeing meaning. Every use of language reveals an order of being that is innately intangible. At the foundation of all of our thinking, communicating, and use of language is a miraculous power. It is the power of noting differences and similarities and of generalizing and universalizing—what the philosophers call concepts, universals, and the like. It is natural to humans, unique, and simply mystifying. How is it that, from childhood, you can effortlessly think of both your dog Caesar and dogs in general? You can think of redness without thinking of a specific red thing (of course redness does not exist independently, but only in red things). You abstract and distinguish and unify without giving your ability to do these things a second thought. And you even ponder things that have no physical characteristics, such as the idea of liberty or the activity of angels. This power of thinking in concepts is by its very nature something that transcends matter.

If there are those who dispute any of this, consistency demands that they stop talking and thinking. Every time they use language, they are illustrating the all-pervasive role of meaning, concepts, intentions, and reason in our lives. And it is simply unintelligible to talk of intellection having a physical counterpart (there is no organ that performs understanding), although, of course, the data provided by the senses provide some of the raw material utilized by thought. Once you think about it for a few minutes, you will know instantly that the idea that your thought of something is in any sense physical will be seen as unthinkably absurd. Let's say you are thinking about a picnic you are planning with your family and friends. You think of different possible locations, people you want to invite, items you want to bring, the vehicle you will use, and the like. Is it coherent to suppose that any of these thoughts are in any sense physically constituted?

The point here is that, strictly speaking, your brain does not understand. You understand. Your brain enables you to understand, but not because your thoughts take place in the brain or because "you" cause certain neurons to fire. Rather, your act of understanding that eliminating poverty is a good thing, to take an instance, is a holistic process that is supraphysical in essence (meaning) and physical in execution (words and neurons). The act cannot be split into supraphysical and physical, because it is an indivisible act of an agent that is intrinsically physical and supraphysical. There is a structure to both the physical and the supraphysical, but their integration is so total that it makes no sense to ask if your acts are physical or supraphysical or even a hybrid of the two. They are acts of a person who is inescapably both embodied and "ensouled."

Many misconceptions about the nature of thought arise from misconceptions about computers. But let's say we're dealing with a supercomputer like the Blue Gene, which does over two hundred trillion calculations per second. Our first mistake is to assume that Blue Gene is an "it" like a bacterium or a bumblebee. In the case of the bacterium or the bumblebee we're dealing with an agent, a center of action that is an organically unified whole, an organism. All its actions are driven by the goals of maintaining itself in existence and replicating. Blue Gene is a bundle of parts that jointly or severally perform functions "implanted" and directed by the creators of the collection.

Second, the bundle of parts does not know what "it" is doing when "it" performs a transaction. Supercomputer calculations and mainframe transactions performed in response to data and instructions are purely and simply a matter of electrical pulses, circuitry, and transistors. The same calculations and transactions performed by a human person, of course, involve the machinery of the brain, but they are performed by a center of consciousness who is conscious of what is going on, understands what is being done, and intentionally performs them. There is no awareness, understanding, meaning, intention, or person involved when the computer performs the same actions, even when the computer has multiple processors operating at superhuman speeds. The output of the computer has "meaning" for us (the weather forecast for tomorrow or your bank balance), but as far as the bundle of parts called the computer is concerned there are binary digits, 0's and 1's, that drive certain mechanical activities. To suggest that the computer "understands" what it is doing is like saying that a power line can meditate on the question of free will and determinism, or that the chemicals in a test tube can apply the principle of noncontradiction in solving a problem, or that a DVD player understands and enjoys the music it plays.

THE SELF

Paradoxically the most important oversight of the new atheists is the most obvious datum of all: themselves. The ultimate supraphysical/physical reality that we know from experience is the experiencer itself, namely, ourselves. Once we acknowledge the fact that there is a first-person perspective, "I," "me," "mine," and the like, we encounter the greatest and yet the most exhilarating mystery of all. I exist. To reverse Descartes, "I am, therefore I think, perceive, intend, mean, interact." Who is this "I"? "Where" is it? How did it come to be? Your self is obviously not just something physical, just as it is not just something supraphysical. It is an embodied self, an ensouled body; "you" are not in a particular brain cell or in some part of your body. The cells in your body keep changing and yet "you" remain the same. If you study your neurons, you will find that none of them have the property of being an "I." Of course your body is integral to who you are, but it is a "body" because it constituted as such by the self. To be human is to be embodied and ensouled.

In a famous passage in his *A Treatise of Human Nature,* Hume declares, "When I enter most intimately into what I call myself, ... I never can catch myself at any time without a perception, and never can observe anything but the perception."[14] Here Hume denies the existence of a self simply by arguing that he (meaning "I"!) can't find "myself." But what is it that unifies his various experiences, that enables him to be aware of the external world, and that remains the same throughout? Who's asking these questions? He assumes that "myself" is an observable state like his thoughts and feelings. But the self is not something that can be thus observed. It is a constant fact of experience and, in fact, the ground of all experience.

Indeed, of all the truths available to us, the self is at the same time the most obvious and unassailable and the most lethal for all forms of physicalism. To begin with, it must be said that a denial of the self cannot even be claimed without contradiction. To the question, "How do I know I exist?" a professor famously replied, "And who's asking?" The self is what we are and not what we have. It is the "I" from which arises our first-person perspective. We cannot analyze the self, because it is not a mental state that can be observed or described.

The most fundamental reality of which we are all aware, then, is the human self, and an understanding of the self inevitably sheds insights on all the origin questions and makes sense of reality as a whole. We realize that the self cannot be described, let alone explained, in terms of physics or chemistry: science does not discover the self; the self discovers science. We realize that no account of the history of the universe is coherent if it cannot account for the existence of the self.

THE ORIGIN OF THE SUPRAPHYSICAL

So how did life, consciousness, thought, and the self come to be? The history of the world shows the sudden emergence of these phenomena—life appearing soon after the cooling of planet earth, consciousness mysteriously manifesting itself in the Cambrian explosion, language emerging in the "symbolic species" without any evolutionary forerunner. The phenomena in question range from code and symbol-processing systems and goal-seeking, intention-manifesting agents at one end to subjective awareness, conceptual thought, and the human self at the other. The only coherent way to describe these phenomena is to say that they are different dimensions of being that are supraphysical in one way or another. They are totally integrated with the physical and yet radically "new." We are not talking here of ghosts in machines, but of agents of different kinds, some that are conscious, others that are both conscious and thinking. In every case there is no vitalism or dualism, but an integration that is total, a holism that incorporates physical and mental.

Although the new atheists have failed to come to grips with either the nature or the source of life, consciousness, thought, and the self, the answer to the question of the origin of the supraphysical seems obvious: the supraphysical can only originate in a supraphysical source. Life, consciousness, mind, and the self can only come from a Source that is living, conscious, and thinking. If we are centers of consciousness and thought who are able to know and love and intend and execute, I cannot see how such centers could come to be from something that is itself incapable of all these activities. Although simple physical processes could create complex physical phenomena, we are not concerned here with the relation of simple and complex, but with the origin of "centers." It's simply inconceivable that any material matrix or field can generate agents who think and act. Matter cannot produce conceptions and perceptions. A force field does not plan or think. So at the level of reason and everyday experience, we become immediately aware that the world of living, conscious, thinking beings has to originate in a living Source, a Mind.

APPENDIX B

The Self-Revelation of God in Human History:
A Dialogue on Jesus with N. T. Wright

ANTONY FLEW:
QUESTIONS ABOUT DIVINE REVELATION

U p to this point I have discussed the data that led me to accept the existence of a divine Mind. Those who hear these arguments almost inevitably ask what I think about the claims of divine revelation. In both my antitheological books and various debates, I have taken issue with many of the claims of divine revelation or intervention.

My current position, however, is more open to at least certain of these claims. In point of fact, I think that the Christian religion is the one religion that most clearly deserves to be honored and respected whether or not its claim to be a divine revelation is true. There is nothing like the combination of a charismatic figure like Jesus and a first-class intellectual like St. Paul. Virtually all the argument about the content of the religion was produced by St. Paul, who had a brilliant philosophical mind and could both speak and write in all the relevant languages. If you're wanting Omnipotence to set up a religion, this is the one to beat.

In early editions of *God and Philosophy,* I addressed the claims of Christianity to some extent. I argued that the enormous advances made in the critical study of the New Testament and other sources for the history of the origins of Christianity meant there is "no place to hide" for those who make wide and large historical claims. Second, the occurrence of miracles cannot be known from historical evidence, and this discredits the claim that the resurrection can be known as a fact of history.

In my various debates on the resurrection of Christ, I made several additional points. First, the most recent documents for the alleged event were written some thirty or more years after it. There is no contemporary evidence— just documents written years afterwards. Second, we have no way of checking whether the risen Jesus actually appeared to groups, since we only have a document alleging that these extraordinary events took place. Finally, the evidence for the resurrection is very limited. In fact, the first New Testament documents on the resurrection were the Letters of Paul and not the Gospels, and these Letters have very little physical detail on the resurrection.

Today, I would say the claim concerning the resurrection is more impressive than any by the religious competition. I still believe that when historians professionally are looking at the evidence, they surely need much more than what is available. They need evidence of a different kind.

I think the claim that God was incarnate in Jesus Christ is unique. It is difficult, I think, to realize how you are going to judge this other than by believing or not believing. I cannot quite see that there are general principles to guide you in this.

In the context of my new perspective, I have engaged in a dialogue on Jesus with a well-known contemporary expounder of historical Christianity, Bishop N. T. Wright of Durham, an Oxford New Testament scholar. Below are his responses to some of the issues I have raised in my writings.

N. T. WRIGHT: RESPONSE

How Do We Know That Jesus Existed?

It is quite difficult to know where to start, because actually the evidence for Jesus is so massive that, as a historian, I want to say we have got almost as much good evidence for Jesus as for anyone in the ancient world. Obviously there are some characters from the ancient world for whom we have statues and inscriptions. On the other hand, we have statues of gods and goddesses in the ancient world too, and so you can never quite be sure. But in Jesus's case, the evidence all points firmly back to the existence of this great figure in the 20s through to around 30 of the first century. And the evidence fits so well with what we know of the Judaism of the period (even though much of it was eventually written down a generation later) that I think there are hardly any historians today, in fact I don't know of any historians today, who doubt the existence of Jesus. There are one or two. A man called [G. A.] Wells is the only one who has made much of it recently. From time to time you get someone like J. M. Allegro, who a generation ago wrote a book on the basis of the Dead Sea Scrolls saying that Christianity was all about a cult of the sacred mushroom. No Jewish, Christian, atheist, or agnostic scholars have ever taken that seriously since. It is quite clear that in fact Jesus is a very, very well documented character of real history. So I think that question can be put to rest.

What Grounds Are There for Claiming, from the Texts, That Jesus Is God Incarnate?

My faith in Jesus as the incarnate Son of God does not rest on the verses in the Gospels making this claim. It goes much deeper, in fact way back to the very important question about how first-century Jews understood God and

God's action in the world. And, of course, as Jews they
went back to the Psalms, to Isaiah, to Deuteronomy, to
Genesis, and so on. And we can see, in the Jewish traditions of Jesus's day, how they interpreted these. They talk
about the one God who has made the world, who is also the
God of Israel, and they talk about this God as active within
the world, present and doing things within the world and
within Israel. And they talk about this in five ways (nothing
to do with Aquinas's Five Ways!).

They talk about the Word of God: God spoke and it was
done; God said, "Let there light," and there was light. The
Word of God is living and active, and in Isaiah we have the
very powerful image of the Word coming down like rain or
snow and doing things in the world.

They talk about the wisdom of God. We see this in
Proverbs, of course, particularly, but in several other passages as well. Wisdom becomes almost a personification,
if you like, of God's "second self." Wisdom is active in the
world, dwelling in Israel, and doing things that help human
beings themselves to be wise.

They talk about the glory of God dwelling in the Temple. We must never forget that for Jews in the first century
the Temple was, so to speak, an incarnational symbol—
they really did believe that the Creator of the universe
had promised to come and make his home in this building
just down the road in Jerusalem. Until you actually go to

Jerusalem and think about that, you don't really realize it. But it's quite extraordinary.

Then, of course, they talk about the law of God, which is perfect and revives the soul (as in Psalm 19). The law, like wisdom, is not just a written law. It is an ontologically existing force and presence through which God makes himself known.

And, then, finally they talk about the Spirit of God. The Spirit of God rushes upon Samson in the book of Judges; the Spirit of God enables the prophets to be prophets; the Spirit of God indwells humans so that they can do extraordinary things for God's glory.

These five ways of speaking about God's action in the world were all ways in which first-century Jews expressed their belief that the One they knew as the Eternal God, the Creator of the world, was present and active within the world and particularly within Israel. And you can see this all over, not just in the Old Testament, but in the footprint that the Old Testament leaves in first-century Judaism, the rabbis, and the Dead Sea Scrolls and other similar texts.

Now when we come to the Gospels with those five ways of speaking in our heads, we discover Jesus behaving—not just talking, but behaving—as if somehow those five ways are coming true in a new manner in what he is doing. In particular, we see this in the parable of the sower. The sower sows the Word, and the Word does its own work.

But, wait a minute, who is going around doing this teaching? It is Jesus himself.

And then likewise Jesus speaks in various ways about wisdom: the wisdom of God says, "I am doing this, I am doing that." And you can track the wisdom traditions of the Old Testament in not just the individual sayings of Jesus, but in the way he went about doing what he was doing. His challenges about the wise man who built his house on the rock and the foolish man who built his house on the sand—that's a typical bit of wisdom teaching. But, wait a minute, the wise man is "the one who hears these words of *mine* and does them." So wisdom and Jesus are very closely bound together.

And then, particularly, the Temple. Jesus behaves as if he is the Temple in person. When he says, "Your sins are forgiven," that is a real shock, because forgiveness of sins is normally declared when you go to the Temple and offer sacrifice. And yet Jesus says you can have it right here out on the street. When you're with Jesus, it's as though you're in the Temple, gazing upon God's glory.

When we come to the Jewish law, we discover something fascinating. One of the great Jewish scholars of our day, Jacob Neusner, who's written several major books on Judaism, wrote a book about Jesus. In it he said that when he reads that Jesus said things like, "You have heard that it was said thus and so, but I say unto you this and this and this," he says, "I want to say to this Jesus: Who do you think you are? God?" Jesus is actually giving a new law, a radically fresh interpretation of the law, and is claiming, in certain respects, to override the way the law was being understood and interpreted.

And, then, finally the Spirit. Jesus says, "If I by the Spirit of God cast out demons, then the Kingdom of God has come upon you."

So what we see is not so much Jesus going around saying, "I am the Second Person of the Trinity. Either believe it or not." That really isn't the way to read the Gospels. Rather, reading them as first-century historians, we can see that Jesus is behaving in ways that together say: this whole great story about a God who comes to be with his people is actually happening. Only it isn't through the Word and wisdom and the rest. It's in and as a person. The thing that draws all this together (I have spelled this out in the penultimate chapter of my book *Jesus and the Victory of God*) is that many Jews of Jesus's day believed that one day Yahweh, the God of Israel, would come back in person to live within the Temple. You find that in Ezekiel, Isaiah, Zechariah, and several of the later postbiblical texts.

So they're hoping that one day God will come back. Because, of course, when God comes back, then he'll send the Romans packing. He will rebuild the Temple properly—not the way in which Herod had been doing it, and so on. There's a string of expectations associated with God's return. And then we find in the Gospels this extraordinary picture of Jesus making a final journey to Jerusalem, *telling stories about the king who comes back.*

I have argued, as others have, that Jesus, in telling those stories about the king who comes back to his people, the master who comes back to his servants, is not talking of some Second Coming way in the future. The disciples weren't up for that. They didn't even know that he was going to be crucified. He's telling stories about the significance of his own journey to Jerusalem, and he's inviting those who have ears to hear to take this Old Testament picture of Yahweh returning to Zion and hold that in their heads as they see him as a young prophet riding into Jerusalem on a donkey.

I think Jesus staked his life—quite literally!—on his belief that he was called to *embody* the return of Yahweh to Zion. Now, *embody* is an English word. The Latin equivalent is *incarnation,* of course. But I prefer to say *embody,* because, at least in the places where I preach, people can relate to this better than to a technical Latin term. But it means the same thing.

I really do believe that Jesus believed that he was called to act on that assumption. And I think that was hugely scary for Jesus. I think he knew he might actually be wrong. After all, some people who believe that sort of thing might turn out to be like the man who believes he's a pot of tea. I think Jesus knew that that was his vocation, that he had to act in that way, to live and act on the basis of a vocation to embody, to incarnate, the return of Israel's God to his people. That's why I would say that Jesus, very quickly after his death and resurrection (that's a whole other story; we'll come to it presently), was recognized by his followers as being, all along, the embodiment of Israel's God. Faced with his resurrection, they then went back in their minds to all the things that they had seen, heard, and known about Jesus and, as it were, slapped themselves on the side of their heads and said, "Do you realize who we have been with all this time? We have been with the one who embodies Israel's God." And they then told and retold the stories of Jesus with awe and wonder as, with hindsight, they reflected on what had been happening all along.

This is a huge, extraordinary idea. Yet it makes deep and historically rooted sense that Jesus should think like that about himself. Now, of course, it would be perfectly open to anyone to say to me, "Well, maybe you're right. Maybe Jesus really did believe that about himself. Maybe the disciples did come to think in that way too. But clearly Jesus must have been wrong, either because we know a priori that if there was a God he could never become human, or because we know a priori that anyone who thinks like that about himself really must have been mad, deranged, deluded."

To this I would say: okay, fine, but just hold those a prioris off for the moment, keep the dogs at bay. And just hold in your mind the picture of a first-century Jew believing and doing all that I have said. And then ask the question about the resurrection. And then ask all the other questions about what we mean by the word *God* anyway. Because, of course, the early Christians said most emphatically that the word *God* remains systematically vague, and that it's only when we look at Jesus that we find it comes into focus. John says, "No one has seen God at any time; but the only begotten Son, who lives in the bosom of the Father, he has made him known." The Greek at this point means, literally, "He has provided an exegesis of him, he has shown us who God really is."

That's a long answer to a vital question, but I don't think I can make it any shorter. Most people, in my experience, don't think through the question of Jesus and God in this way. But this is how, I think, Jesus himself, the earliest Christians, and those who wrote the Gospels were thinking, and we do well to get our minds around it.

What Evidence Is There for the Resurrection of Christ?

Let me make this as short as I can. My father read my long book, *The Resurrection of the Son of God*, when he was eighty-three. It took him three days to read seven hundred pages. He read right through it; he just did nothing else. He phoned me up and said, "I've finished it." And I said, "You what?" He said, "Yes. And I really started to enjoy it after about page 600." I thought it was a wonderfully back-handed compliment. My father used to be in the timber business. I said, "Dad, you need to know that the first five hundred or so pages are the root system. And if the tree doesn't have a root system, it won't be able to stand up and it won't bear any fruit." And he said, "Yes, I sort of fig-ured that out. But I always preferred the upper branches myself."

So I need to delve into the root system a bit. One of the things I really enjoyed when I wrote that book was going back to my classical stomping grounds and researching ancient beliefs about life after death, Greek and Roman and Egyp-tian beliefs about life after death. And there's a huge range of beliefs about life after death, but "resurrection" doesn't feature in the Greco-Roman world. In fact, Pliny, Aeschylus, Homer, Cicero, and all sorts of early writers say, "Of course, we know resurrection doesn't happen." Now, at the same time, the Jews had developed quite a specific theology about resurrection: that God's people would be bodily raised from the dead at the end of time. The time element is very impor-tant, because most Christians in the Western world use the word *resurrection* as a vague word to mean "life after death," which it never did in the ancient world. It was always a very specific term for what I call life *after* life after death. In other words, first you die, you are dead and not bodily alive, and then you are "resurrected," which means you begin a new bodily life, a new life *after* whatever "life after death" may consist of.

We can track the way in which *resurrection* belief occurs in Judaism. Resurrection is a two-stage sequence: right after you die you're immediately in this holding pattern or waiting state; and then you have this entirely new life called *resurrection*. Now, in the book I had great fun drawing a map of Jewish beliefs in life after death on the larger map of ancient beliefs in life after death in general. And within Judaism itself there are additional variations. The Pharisees believed in resurrection, and this seems to have been the majority belief in Palestinian Judaism at the time of Jesus. The Sadducees didn't believe in life after death at all, certainly not resurrection. And people like Philo and perhaps the Essenes (though that's controversial) believed in a single-stage disembodied immortality, in which, after death, you simply go wherever you are going and stay there, rather than experiencing a subsequent resurrection.

Now, this is all the more interesting because, in all the societies that have been studied in this respect, beliefs about life after death are very conservative. Faced with death, people tend to lurch back to beliefs and practices they know, to where they came from, to how their tradition, their family, their village, and so on, has always done burial customs. So it is truly remarkable that all the early Christians known to us, right through till the late second century when the Gnostics start to use the word *resurrection* in quite a different sense (but we'll leave that aside)— all the early Christians known to us for the first four or five generations believed in a future bodily resurrection, even though most of them came from the pagan world, where this was regarded as complete and utter rubbish.

A modern myth circulating at the moment says that it's only we who have contemporary post-Enlightenment science who have discovered that dead people don't rise. Those people back then, poor things, were unenlightened, so they believed in all these crazy miracles. But that is simply false. A lovely quote by C. S. Lewis relates to this. He is talking about the virginal conception of Jesus and says that the reason Joseph was worried about Mary's pregnancy was not because he didn't know where babies come from, but because he did. It's the same with the resurrection of Jesus. People in the ancient world were incredulous when faced with the Christian claim, because they knew perfectly well that when people die they stay dead.

And what we then find—and this to me is utterly fascinating—that we can track, in early Christianity, several modifications in the classic Jewish belief about resurrection. First, instead of resurrection being something that was simply going to happen to all God's people at the end, the early Christians said it had happened to one person in advance. Now, no first-century Jew, as far as we know, believed there would be one person raised ahead of everybody else. So that's a radical innovation, but they all believed that.

Second, they believed that resurrection would involve the *transformation* of the physical body. Those Jews who believed in resurrection seem to have gone in one of two directions. Some said it would produce a physical body exactly like this one all over again, and others said it would be a luminous body, one shining like a star. The early Christians didn't say either of those things. They talked about a new sort of physicality—this is very clear in Paul, but not only in Paul—a new type of embodiedness that is definitely bodily in the sense of being solid and substantial, but seems to have been transformed so that it is now not susceptible to pain or suffering or death. And this is quite new. That picture of resurrection is not in Judaism.

Third, of course, they believed that the Messiah himself had been raised from the dead, which no Second Temple Jew believed because, according to Second Temple Judaism, the Messiah was never going to be killed. So that was novel.

Fourth, they used the idea of "resurrection" in quite
new ways. In Judaism, the idea had been used as a meta-
phor for "return from exile," as we find in Ezekiel 37. But
within early Christianity—and I mean very early Christianity, for example, Paul—we find it being used in connection with baptism, holiness, and various other aspects
of Christian living that were not in mind within Judaism
and its use of "resurrection." This again shows quite a
radical innovation, a mutation from its form in the Jewish
viewpoint.

Fifth, we find that for the earliest Christians "resurrection" comes to be thought of as something to which God's
people in the present actually contribute. Christians are
called to work together with God to implement what was
launched at Easter and so to anticipate the new world God
will make eventually. This too is quite new, but only expli-
cable as a mutation within Judaism.

Sixth, we find that in early Christianity "resurrection"
has moved from being one doctrine among many others—
important, but not that important—which is where it is
in Judaism, to become the center of everything. Take it
away from Paul, say, or 1 Peter, Revelation, or the great
second-century fathers, and you will destroy their whole
framework. We have to conclude that something must have
happened to bring "resurrection" in from the periphery to
the center, to the focal point.

Seventh, and finally, we find that in early Christianity there is virtually no spectrum of belief about what happens after death. In Judaism there were several different viewpoints, and in the pagan world there were a great many, but in early Christianity there was only one: resurrection itself. Granted how conservative most people are in their views about life after death, this is truly remarkable. It really does look as though the earliest Christians had good reason to rethink even this most personal and important point of belief. And when we look at the spectrum of early Christianity, we see that the early Christians disagreed about quite a lot of things, but they are remarkably unanimous in their view not only of resurrection as their belief, but of how resurrection plays out and how it works. All this is spelled out in my book in great detail.

All this forces us as historians to ask a very simple question: Why did all the early Christians known to us, from the earliest times for which we have evidence, have this very new, but remarkably unanimous, view of resurrection? That is a genuinely interesting historical question in its own right. Of course, all the early Christians known to us would say, "We have this view of resurrection because of what we believe about Jesus." Now, if the idea that Jesus had been raised from the dead only started to crop up after twenty or thirty years of Christianity, as many skeptical scholars have supposed, you would find lots of strands of early Christianity in which there really wasn't much place for resurrection—or, if you did find resurrection, it might have a different shape from the very specific one it has in early Christianity. Therefore, the wide extent and unanimity of early Christian belief in resurrection force us to say that something definite *happened*, way back early on, that has shaped and colored the whole early Christian movement.

At that point we have to say, "All right then, what about the Gospel narratives?" What about Matthew 28, that short narrative in Mark 16 and the longer one in Luke 24, and the much longer one in John 20–21? And, of course, I, like virtually all Gospel scholars, believe that those were written down much later. I don't actually know when the Gospels were written. Nobody knows that, although scholars keep on telling us they know. They could have been written as early as the 50s of the first century; some would say even earlier. They could have been written as late as the 70s or 80s; some would even say the 90s. But for my argument at the moment this doesn't matter at all.

The point is this: The Gospel resurrection narratives (and the related material at the start of Acts) have certain key features, common to all four of them, demonstrating historically that, though they were written down later, they go back in a way that has not been altered very much at all, lightly edited but not substantially altered, to very early oral tradition. This is, obviously, of huge importance.

The first feature is the portrait of Jesus in the resurrection narratives. It has been said again and again (and when I was researching the big book I got very tired of reading scholars saying this) that (1) Mark was written first, and he's hardly got anything about the resurrection; (2) Matthew comes next, and there's not much more; and then (3) toward the end of the century we get Luke and John, and then and only then do we find stories about Jesus eating broiled fish, cooking breakfast by the shore, inviting Thomas to touch him, and so on. According to the theory, then, there were Christians toward the end of the century who started to believe that Jesus wasn't really truly human, that he wasn't really a true man, and so Luke and John make up these stories at that stage in order to say, yes, he really was human, the risen Jesus really had bodily form, and so on.

The trouble with that theory—which, as I say, has been very popular—is that those narratives (about Jesus cooking breakfast by the shore, breaking the bread at Emmaus, inviting Thomas to touch him, and so on) have this same Jesus coming and going through locked doors, sometimes being recognized and sometimes not being recognized, appearing and disappearing at will, and finally ascending to heaven. Let me put it like this. If I were making up a narrative in, say, 95 C.E. because I knew that some of my folk were a little insecure on the question of whether Jesus was a really solid human being, I wouldn't put all that material in. It's a kind of "own goal."

From the other point of view, if you were a first-century Jew wanting to invent a story about Jesus being raised from the dead, the natural biblical source for you to draw on would be Daniel 12, which is one of the big texts on resurrection for Second Temple Judaism. Daniel 12 says that the righteous will shine like stars in the kingdom of their Father. In fact, Jesus quotes that in an earlier passage in Matthew 13. It is therefore all the more fascinating that none of the resurrection narratives have Jesus shining like a star. He should have done so if they were making it up from the text.

Thus, from these two points of view, the portrait of Jesus in the resurrection narratives is very, very odd. It's not what you would expect. There is no portrait like that in the Jewish narratives of the time. And yet, remarkably, it is consistent across Matthew and Luke and John. (Mark is too short for us to know what he might have said if he had gone on.) So something very odd has happened. It sounds as though the Evangelists are trying to say to us, "I know you're going to find it very difficult to believe, but this is actually what happened." Something extraordinary has happened that's left its footprints in the narratives. People would not have made these things up off the tops of their heads. Anyone writing fictitious accounts of Easter would have made Jesus more clearly recognizable.

Let me say something here as an aside. If you take the resurrection narratives in Matthew, Mark, Luke, and John in the original Greek and compare them side by side, they're quite different—even when they're telling the same bit of the story about the women going to the tomb and so on. They use different words again and again. So it looks as though they haven't simply copied it from each other.

The second thing is that there's an almost complete absence of echo and allusion to the Old Testament in the resurrection narratives. In the crucifixion narratives, it's clear that the story of Jesus's death has been told again and again by the early Christian community, and it's woven Psalm 22, Isaiah 53, Zechariah, and other Old Testament allusions into the crucifixion narrative, even into the burial narrative. But then you turn over the page to the resurrection narrative, and you don't find this in Matthew, Mark, Luke, or John. (And we remind ourselves that Paul has already said in 1 Corinthians 15 that Christ was raised from the dead *"according to the scriptures,"*—Paul already in the early 50s had a rich arsenal of Old Testament texts with which to interpret the resurrection.) It would have been very easy for Matthew, who loves telling us about the fulfillment of Scripture, to say, "This happened in order that the Scripture might be fulfilled that said ... " But Matthew doesn't do that. Similarly, John says that when the disciples went to the tomb, they didn't yet know the scripture that he must be raised from the dead. But he doesn't actually quote the scripture or tell us which it was. And, on the road to Emmaus, Luke has Jesus expounding the Scriptures—but, again, Luke never tells us which scriptures or what Jesus said about them.

This is very odd. Either we have to say that the early church wrote resurrection narratives replete with reflection on the Old Testament and that Matthew, Mark, Luke, and John went through independently and took those references out, or we have to say that these stories go back substantially to an early oral tradition that precedes the theological and exegetical reflection. In my judgment the second of these is far and away the more likely.

The third fascinating feature of the narratives is the place of the women. (This is well known; the point is not original to me.) In the ancient world, Jewish and pagan, women were not credible witnesses in the law court. And already by the time Paul is quoting the public tradition about Jesus in 1 Corinthians 15, he is saying: "Here's the story the way we told it. He was crucified for our sins, according to the scriptures, raised on the third day, according to the scriptures, and then he was seen by ..."—then he has a list of men—"Cephas, by James, by the other early disciples, by five hundred at once, last of all by me." We put up our hands and say, "Excuse me, Paul, where are the women?" The answer is that, already in the early 50s, the public tradition has airbrushed the women out of the account, because the public tradition knew that they were going to be in trouble. We see the trouble they had when we read Celsus, who a century later pours scorn on the resurrection by saying, "This faith is just based on the testimony of some hysterical women."

So it's fascinating that in Matthew, Mark, Luke, and John we have Mary Magdalene, the other Marys, and the other women. And Mary Magdalene, of all people (we know she had a very checkered career in the past), is chosen as the prime witness: there she is in all four accounts. As historians we are obliged to comment that if these stories had been made up five years later, let alone thirty, forty, or fifty years later, they would never have had Mary Magdalene in this role. To put Mary there is, from the point of view of Christian apologists wanting to explain to a skeptical audience that Jesus really did rise from the dead, like shooting themselves in the foot. But to us as historians this kind of thing is gold dust. *The early Christians would never, never have made this up.* The stories—of the women finding an empty tomb and then meeting the risen Jesus—must be regarded as solidly historical.

So to the fourth and final fascinating feature of the accounts. Here I speak as a preacher who has preached pretty much every Easter Day for the last thirty-five years. Preachers in the Western tradition who, at Easter, preach about Jesus rising from the dead tend to preach about our own future life, our own resurrection, or our own going to heaven. But in the resurrection narratives in Matthew, Mark, Luke, and John, there's nothing about our future life. By contrast, almost every time Paul mentions the resurrection, he is making a point about our own future life as well. In Hebrews we're told about Jesus's resurrection and our future resurrection; in the book of Revelation, again, we find the link made between our resurrection and Jesus's resurrection. Justin Martyr, Ignatius of Antioch, and Irenaeus, right across the tradition, all agree: "We think about Jesus's resurrection in order to reflect upon our own."

But Matthew, Mark, Luke, and John don't say, "Jesus is raised, therefore we'll be raised one day." They say—and this often comes as a surprise to people: "Jesus is raised—therefore he really was the Messiah. God's new creation has begun. We've got a job to do. And, what's more, we find ourselves drawn to worship this Jesus, because we find that he has embodied Israel's God, the creator of the universe." In other words, those stories, as we find them in the Gospels, go back to a primitive way of telling the story that hasn't even gotten around yet to saying, "Christ is risen, therefore we will be raised," as we find it solidly in Paul right through from the late 40s. So we have to conclude that these narratives go back way behind Paul to a time when we see the very, very early church reeling in shock from this totally unexpected event of the resurrection and figuring out what it means.

From all this I reach certain conclusions. In order to explain the rise of early Christianity, in order to explain the existence of those four resurrection accounts plus the bits and pieces in Acts and in Paul, we have to say that the very early church really did believe that Jesus had been bodily raised from the dead. We have no evidence of any very early Christians who believed anything else. But how can we as historians explain that?

Obviously, as a Christian you can short-circuit this argument at any point. Many Christians have done that, which is a shame, actually, because they miss the vital point. Often people say, "Of course, he was the Son of God. He could have done anything. Stands to reason, doesn't it?"

But I don't want to do that. I want to be faithful to the texts themselves, which don't say that. We have to ask: How do we explain this extraordinary phenomenon, the fact of early Christianity arising in the first place, taking its very specific shape, and telling the very specific stories that it did? I discover, as I look for historical explanations, that two particular things must have happened: (1) there must have been an empty tomb that was known to be the correct tomb; it couldn't have been a mistake; (2) there must have been appearances of the risen Jesus. Both of these must have occurred.

Why? Because if there had been an empty tomb and no appearances, everybody in the ancient world would have drawn the obvious conclusion (obvious to them even if not to us): body snatchers. Tombs were regularly robbed, especially if the people were rich or famous; there might be jewels in there, there might be something worth stealing. So they would have said what Mary said: "They've taken away the body. I don't know what's happened to it." They would never ever have talked about resurrection, if all that had happened was an empty tomb.

Equally, you cannot explain the historical data we have looked at simply by saying that the disciples must have had some sort of experience they took to be a meeting with Jesus. They knew Jesus had been killed. But they all knew about hallucinations and ghosts and visions. Ancient literature—Jewish and pagan alike—is full of such things. It goes back to Homer; it's in Virgil; it's all over the place. Recently some people have tried to say, by way of arguing that the resurrection couldn't have happened, something like this: "Ah, well, when those you love die, sometimes you will experience them in the room with you, smiling at you, maybe even talking to you; and then they will disappear again. Maybe that's what happened to these disciples." And it's true; I've read some of the literature about that. This is a well-documented phenomenon as part of the grief process, and you can explain it how you like. But the crunch is that *the early Christians knew about phenomena like that as well.* They knew perfectly well that there were such things as visions, hallucinations, dreams, ghosts, and so on. In other words, if they'd had an experience, however vivid it seemed, of being with Jesus, but if the tomb had not been empty, they would have said, "My goodness, this was very powerful, and quite consoling in a way; but he hasn't been raised from the dead, of course, because dead people don't get raised (until all the dead are raised at the end)—and anyway, there is his body in the tomb."

At this point we need to remind ourselves of the way Jews buried people in those days. Most Jewish burials in Palestine at the time were done in the two-stage method. First, you wrap up the body in cloth, with plenty of spices, and place it on a ledge in a rock tomb or perhaps even in the basement of a house. You don't "bury" it the way people do in the modern Western world, in a grave dug in the earth and then filled in, because you would be coming back to pick up the bones once all the flesh had decomposed. (That's why you had spices, because of the smell of decomposition; you wouldn't go to the trouble and expense of spices if you were putting the body underground.) Then, when all the flesh had decomposed, you would collect the bones, fold them up, and put them in an ossuary, a bone box, which you would store either in a loculus (a little niche at the back of the tomb) or in some other convenient place. Archaeologists keep digging up ossuaries in Jerusalem—dozens of them—every time a new road, a new Hilton Hotel, or a new housing estate is built. Archaeologists have hundreds, even thousands, of them.

The point is this. If the body of Jesus had still been in the tomb, the disciples could easily have found out. Then they would have said, "However strong these hallucinations are that we've been having, he hasn't been raised from the dead." So we as historians have to say that there really must have been an empty tomb and there really must have been sightings or, if you like, meetings with somebody discovered to be Jesus, even though he seemed to be strangely transformed in ways they weren't expecting and ways we as readers find quite confusing.

We come at last to the final move in the chess game. How, as a historian, do I explain these two facts, as I take them to be: the empty tomb and the appearances and visions of Jesus. The easiest explanation by far is that these things happened because Jesus really was raised from the dead, and the disciples really did meet him, even though his body was renewed and transformed so that now it seemed to be able to live in two dimensions at once. (That, indeed, is perhaps the best way to understand the phenomena: Jesus was now living in God's dimension and ours, or, if you like, heaven and earth, simultaneously.)

The resurrection of Jesus does in fact provide a *sufficient* explanation for the empty tomb and the meetings with Jesus. Having examined all the other possible hypotheses I've read about anywhere in the literature, I think it's also a *necessary* explanation.

ANTONY FLEW: CONCLUDING REFLECTIONS

I am very much impressed with Bishop Wright's approach, which is absolutely fresh. He presents the case for Christianity as something new for the first time. This is enormously important, especially in the United Kingdom, where the Christian religion has virtually disappeared. It is absolutely wonderful, absolutely radical, and very powerful.

Is it possible that there has been or can be divine revelation? As I said, you cannot limit the possibilities of omnipotence except to produce the logically impossible. Everything else is open to omnipotence.

NOTES

PREFACE

1. Sir Alfred Ayer, "The Existence of the Soul," in *Great Thinkers on Great Questions,* ed. Roy Abraham Varghese (Oxford: OneWorld, 1998), 49.
2. "Modernizing the Case for God," *Time,* April 7, 1980.
3. Richard Dawkins, *The God Delusion* (London: Bantam, 2006), 140.
4. Lewis Wolpert, *Six Impossible Things Before Breakfast* (London: Faber and Faber, 2006), 217.
5. Daniel Dennett, "Living on the Edge," *Inquiry* 1/2 (1993): 141.
6. Dawkins, *The God Delusion,* 58–59.
7. Dawkins, *The God Delusion,* 82.
8. Richard Dawkins, *What We Believe but Cannot Prove,* ed. John Brockman (London: Pocket Books, 2005), 9.
9. Julia Vitullo-Martin, "A Scientist's Scientist," http://www.templeton.org/milestones/milestones_2006–04.asp.
10. Dawkins, *The God Delusion,* 355.
11. Katharine Tait, *My Father, Bertrand Russell* (New York: Harcourt Brace Jovanovich, 1975), 189.
12. Bertrand Russell, *The Autobiography of Bertrand Russell* (London: George Allen and Unwin, 1967), 146.
13. J. H. Muirhead, ed., *Contemporary British Philosophy,* vol. 1 (London: George Allen and Unwin, 1924), 79.
14. J. N. Findlay, "Can God's Existence Be Disproved?" in *New Essays in Philosophical Theology,* ed. Antony Flew and Alasdair MacIntyre (New York: Macmillan, 1955), 47.
15. The report of Hawking's conversations with the driver of his special-needs vehicle, Saul Pasternak, an Orthodox Jew, are found in

"The Driver of Mister Hawking," an article in the Hebrew weekly newspaper *Jerusalem,* December 22, 2006, p. 28. I am indebted to my friend the Israeli physicist and author Gerald Schroeder for bringing this to my attention.

16. Albert Einstein, *The Quotable Einstein*, ed. Alice Calaprice (Princeton, NJ: Princeton University Press, 2005), 238.

Chapter 1

THE CREATION OF AN ATHEIST

1. G. E. M. Anscombe, *The Collected Papers of G. E. M. Anscombe,* vol. 2, *Metaphysics and the Philosophy of Mind* (Minneapolis: University of Minnesota Press, 1981), x.

Chapter 2

WHERE THE EVIDENCE LEADS

1. Michael Dummett, *Truth and Other Enigmas* (Cambridge, MA: Harvard University Press, 1978), 431.

2. I. M. Crombie, "The Possibility of Theological Statements," in *Faith and Logic,* ed. Basil Mitchell (London: Allen & Unwin), 50.

3. Crombie, "The Possibility of Theological Statements," 73, 72.

4. Raeburne Heimbeck, *Theology and Meaning* (London: Allen & Unwin, 1969), 123, 163.

5. Eric L. Mascall, *The Openness of Being* (Philadelphia: Westminster, 1971), 63.

6. J. L. Mackie, *The Miracle of Theism* (Oxford: Clarendon, 1982), 1.

7. Frederick C. Copleston, *Philosophers and Philosophies* (London: Search Press, 1976), 76.

8. Anthony Kenny, *Faith and Reason* (New York: Columbia University Press, 1983), 86.

9. Kai Nielsen, review of *The Presumption of Atheism* by Antony Flew, *Religious Studies Review* 3 (July 1977): 147.

Chapter 3

ATHEISM CALMLY CONSIDERED

1. Gerald Schroeder, "Has Science Discovered God?" http://science. lenicam.com.
2. Richard Dawkins, *The Selfish Gene* (New York: Oxford University Press, 1976), x.

Chapter 4

A PILGRIMAGE OF REASON

1. Albert Einstein, *Out of My Later Years* (New York: Philosophical Library, 1950), 58.
2. David Conway, *The Rediscovery of Wisdom* (London: Macmillan, 2000), 74.
3. Conway, *The Rediscovery of Wisdom*, 2–3.

Chapter 5

WHO WROTE THE LAWS OF NATURE?

1. Stephen Hawking, *A Brief History of Time* (New York: Bantam, 1988), 175, 174.
2. Gregory Benford, "Leaping the Abyss: Stephen Hawking on Black Holes, Unified Field Theory and Marilyn Monroe," *Reason* 4.02 (April 2002): 29.
3. Albert Einstein, quoted in Timothy Ferris, *Coming of Age in the Milky Way* (New York: Morrow, 1988), 177.
4. Antony Flew, *God and Philosophy* (New York: Dell, 1966), 15.
5. Max Jammer, *Einstein and Religion* (Princeton, NJ: Princeton University Press, 1999), 44.
6. Jammer, *Einstein and Religion*, 45.
7. Jammer, *Einstein and Religion*, 45–46.
8. Jammer, *Einstein and Religion*, 48.
9. Jammer, *Einstein and Religion*, 150.

10. Jammer, *Einstein and Religion*, 51.

11. Jammer, *Einstein and Religion*, 148.

12. Albert Einstein, *Lettres a Maurice Solovine reproduits en facsimile et traduits en francais* (Paris: Gauthier-Vilars, 1956), 102–3.

13. Albert Einstein, *Ideas and Opinions*, trans. Sonja Bargmann (New York: Dell, 1973), 49.

14. Einstein, *Ideas and Opinions*, 255.

15. Jammer, *Einstein and Religion*, 93.

16. Albert Einstein, *The Quotable Einstein*, ed. Alice Calaprice (Princeton, NJ: Princeton University Press, 2005), 195–6.

17. For the most part, these quotations are taken from Roy Abraham Varghese, *The Wonder of the World* (Fountain Hills, AZ: Tyr, 2003).

18. Werner Heisenberg, *Across the Frontiers*, trans. Peter Heath (San Francisco: Harper & Row, 1974), 213.

19. Werner Heisenberg, *Physics and Beyond* (San Francisco: Harper & Row, 1971), excerpted in Timothy Ferris, ed., *The World Treasury of Physics, Astronomy and Mathematics* (New York: Little, Brown, 1991), 826.

20. Erwin Schrödinger, *My View of the World* (Cambridge: Cambridge University Press, 1964), 93.

21. Max Planck, *Where Is Science Going?* trans. James Murphy (New York: Norton, 1977), 168.

22. Max Planck, quoted in Charles C. Gillespie, ed., *Dictionary of Scientific Biography* (New York: Scribner, 1975), 15.

23. Paul A. M. Dirac, "The Evolution of the Physicist's Picture of Nature," *Scientific American* 208, no. 5 (May 1963): 53.

24. Charles Darwin, *The Autobiography of Charles Darwin 1809-1882*, ed. Nora Barlow (London: Collins, 1958), 92–3.

25. Paul Davies, Templeton Prize Address, May 1995, http://aca. mq.edu.au/PaulDavies/prize_address.htm. See also Davies's "Where Do the Laws of Physics Come From?" (2006), http://www. ctnsstars.org/conferences/papers/Wheredothelawsofphysicscome-from.doc.

26. John Barrow, Templeton Prize Address, March 15, 2006, http:// www.templetonprize.org/barrow_statement.html.

27. John Foster, *The Divine Lawmaker: Lectures on Induction, Laws of Nature and the Existence of God* (Oxford: Clarendon, 2004), 160.

28. Richard Swinburne, "Design Defended," *Think* (Spring 2004): 14.
29. Paul Davies, "What Happened Before the Big Bang?" in *God for the 21st Century*, ed. Russell Stannard (Philadelphia: Templeton Foundation Press, 2000), 12.

Chapter 6

DID THE UNIVERSE KNOW WE WERE COMING?

1. Freeman J. Dyson, *Disturbing the Universe* (New York: Harper & Row, 1979), 250. Also cited in John Barrow and Frank Tipler, *The Anthropic Cosmological Principle* (Oxford: Clarendon, 1988), 318.
2. John Leslie, *Infinite Minds* (Oxford: Clarendon, 2001), 213.
3. Leslie, *Infinite Minds*, 203–5.
4. Martin J. Rees, "Numerical Coincidences and 'Tuning' in Cosmology," *Astrophysics and Space Science* 285 (2003): 376.
5. Rees, "Numerical Coincidences and 'Tuning' in Cosmology," 385.
6. Paul Davies, "Universes Galore: Where Will It All End?" http://aca.mq.edu.au/PaulDavies/publications/chapters/Universesgalore.pdf.
7. Richard Swinburne, "Design Defended," *Think* (Spring 2004): 17.
8. Rees, "Numerical Coincidences and 'Tuning' in Cosmology," 386.
9. Davies, "Universes Galore: Where Will It All End?"
10. Martin Rees, "Exploring Our Universe and Others," in *The Frontiers of Space* (New York: Scientific American, 2000), 87.

Chapter 7

HOW DID LIFE GO LIVE?

1. Antony Flew, *God and Philosophy* (Amherst, NY: Prometheus, 2005), 11.
2. Richard Cameron, "Aristotle on the Animate: Problems and Prospects," *Bios: Epistemological and Philosophical Foundation of Life Sciences,* Rome, February 23–24, 2006.
3. John Haldane, "Preface to the Second Edition," in *Atheism and Theism* (Great Debates in Philosophy), J. J. C. Smart and John Haldane (Oxford: Blackwell, 2003), 224.
4. David Conway, *The Rediscovery of Wisdom* (London: Macmillan, 2000), 125.

5. David Berlinski, "On the Origins of Life," *Commentary* (February 2006): 25, 30–31.

6. Carl Woese, "Translation: In Retrospect and Prospect," *RNA* (2001): 1061, 1056, 1064.

7. Paul Davies, "The Origin of Life II: How Did It Begin?" http://aca.mq.edu.au/PaulDavies/publications/papers/OriginsOfLife_II.pdf.

8. Andy Knoll, PBS *Nova* interview, May 3, 2004.

9. Antonio Lazcano, "The Origins of Life," *Natural History* (February 2006).

10. John Maddox, *What Remains to Be Discovered* (New York: Touchstone, 1998), 252.

11. George Wald, "Life and Mind in the Universe," in *Cosmos, Bios, Theos*, ed. Henry Margenau and Roy Abraham Varghese (La Salle, IL: Open Court, 1992), 218.

Chapter 8

DID SOMETHING COME FROM NOTHING?

1. "Something Good," music and lyrics by Richard Rodgers, 1965.

2. Stephen Hawking, *A Brief History of Time* (New York: Bantam, 1988), 174.

3. Antony Flew, "Stephen Hawking and the Mind of God" (1996), http://www.infidels.org/library/modern/antony_flew/hawking.html.

4. Hawking, *A Brief History of Time*, 9.

5. Antony Flew, "The Legitimation of Factual Necessity," in *Faith, Scepticism and Personal Identity*, ed. J. J. MacIntosh and H. A. Meynell (Alberta: University of Calgary Press, 1994), 111–17.

6. David Conway, *The Rediscovery of Wisdom* (London: Macmillan, 2000), 111–12.

7. Richard Swinburne, *The Existence of God* (Oxford: Clarendon, 2004), 142.

8. Richard Swinburne, "The Limits of Explanation," in *Explanation and Its Limits*, ed. Dudley Knowles (Cambridge: Cambridge University Press, 1990), 178–79.

9. John Leslie, *Infinite Minds* (Oxford: Clarendon, 2001), 194–95.

10. Stephen Hawking, *Black Holes and Baby Universes* (New York: Bantam, 1993), 172.

11. Leslie, *Infinite Minds,* 193–94.

12. Swinburne, *The Existence of God,* 152.

Chapter 9
FINDING SPACE FOR GOD

1. John Gaskin, "Gods, Ghosts and Curious Persons," unpublished paper.

2. Thomas F. Tracy, *God, Action and Embodiment* (Grand Rapids, MI: Eerdmans, 1984), 147, 153. See also *The God Who Acts,* ed. Thomas F. Tracy (University Park: Pennsylvania State University Press, 1994).

3. Brian Leftow, personal conversation with the author, Oriel College, Oxford University, October 2006.

4. David Conway, *The Rediscovery of Wisdom* (London: Macmillan, 2000), 134.

APPENDIX A: THE "NEW ATHEISM"

1. Hao Wang, *A Logical Journey: From Gödel to Philosophy* (Cambridge, MA: MIT Press, 1996), 316.

2. Palle Yourgrau, *A World Without Time: The Forgotten Legacy of Gödel and Einstein* (New York: Basic Books, 2005), 104–5.

3. Daniel Dennett, *Breaking the Spell* (New York: Viking, 2006), 244.

4. Anthony Zee, *Fearful Symmetry* (New York: Macmillan, 1986), 280–81.

5. J. J. C. Smart and John Haldane, *Atheism and Theism* (Great Debates in Philosophy) (Oxford: Blackwell, 2003), 228 ff.

6. Howard H. Pattee, "The Physics of Symbols: Bridging the Epistemic Cut," *Biosystems* 60 (2001): 5–21.

7. Lewis Wolpert, *Six Impossible Things Before Breakfast* (London: Faber and Faber, 2006), 212–13.

8. Richard Dawkins, *The God Delusion* (London: Bantam, 2006), 137.

9. Dawkins, *The God Delusion,* 137–38.

10. John Searle, *The Rediscovery of the Mind* (Cambridge, MA: MIT Press, 1992), 9.

11. Sam Harris, *The End of Faith* (New York: Norton, 2004), 208–9.

12. Richard Dawkins and Steven Pinker, "Is Science Killing the Soul?"
    The Guardian-Dillons Debate, *Edge* 53 (April 8, 1999).
13. Wolpert, *Six Impossible Things Before Breakfast,* 78.
14. David Hume, *A Treatise of Human Nature,* edited and with an
    introduction by Ernest C. Mossner (Hammondsworth, Middlesex:
    Penguin Books, 1985), 300.